MINING
YOUR CLIENT'S
METAPHORS

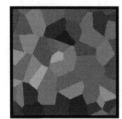

MINING
YOUR CLIENT'S
METAPHORS

A How-to Workbook on
Clean Language and
Symbolic Modeling

BASICS PART ONE:
FACILITATING CLARITY

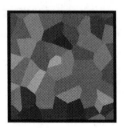

Gina Campbell

BALBOA.PRESS

A DIVISION OF HAY HOUSE

Balboa Press books may be ordered through booksellers or by contacting:

Balboa Press
A Division of Hay House
1663 Liberty Drive
Bloomington, IN 47403
www.balboapress.com
844-682-1282

Because of the dynamic nature of the Internet, any web addresses or links contained in
this book may have changed since publication and may no longer be valid. The views
expressed in this work are solely those of the author and do not necessarily reflect the views
of the publisher, and the publisher hereby disclaims any responsibility for them.

The author of this book does not dispense medical advice or prescribe the use of any technique as a form
of treatment for physical, emotional, or medical problems without the advice of a physician, either directly
or indirectly. The intent of the author is only to offer information of a general nature to help you in your quest
for emotional and spiritual well-being. In the event you use any of the information in this book for yourself,
which is your constitutional right, the author and the publisher assume no responsibility for your actions.

Any people depicted in stock imagery provided by Thinkstock are models,
and such images are being used for illustrative purposes only.
Certain stock imagery © Thinkstock.

ISBN: 978-1-4525-5875-2 (sc)
ISBN: 978-1-4525-5874-5 (e)

Print information available on the last page.

Balboa Press rev. date: 10/21/2021

First Edition

Find us on the Internet at www.miningyourmetaphors.com

How-To Workbooks
BASICS: PARTS I and II

Clean Language

Symbolic Modeling

Modeling Strategies   Metaphors

BASICS PART I: **Facilitating Clarity**

9 Clean Language Questions about:

- **Attributes**
- **Getting a Metaphor**
- **Desired Outcomes**
- **Location**
- **Time and Sequence**
- **Relationship**

What is Clean Language?
What is Symbolic Modeling?
Structuring a Session start to finish
Facilitation Techniques
Clean Space experience
Working from a Metaphor Map/Drawing

BASICS PART II: Facilitating Change

3+ Clean Language Questions about:

- Conditions for Change
- Maturing a Change
- 20 Specialized Questions
- Creating Your Own Specialized CLQs

The Five-Stage Process
Enriching Part I material
Modeling Strategy
Scope of Practice: Counseling and Coaching

Acknowledgments

Starting with the developers of Symbolic Modeling, James Lawley and Penny Tompkins, everyone I've met in the Clean Language community has been generous in sharing their skills, ideas, and materials. I am indebted particularly to Penny and James, and to Wendy Sullivan, Judy Rees, Phil Swallow, Caitlin Walker and others from whom I have learned so much and been so inspired. I'm also very appreciative for the contributions made by Rosemary Scavullo-Flickinger, Zaba Walker and Johannes Walker to my thinking on training. As for this workbook, again thank you to Penny and James for your careful reading and suggestions, and much appreciation to Peggy O. Heller, Chaddie Hughes, Judi Grunwald, Brett C.A. Welch, and all my trainees, whose feedback over the years has improved this book immeasurably. I appreciate your wisdom and creativity with all things Clean!

Gina Campbell

Welcome

It seems that most people who determine to study Clean Language and Symbolic Modeling, who want to really master the techniques, come with a story. There was some Aha! moment of experience when they realized this is something different, something very special, and this way of thinking, of connecting with, and of guiding others would be an invaluable tool in their work.

My story began when I stumbled upon Tompkins and Lawley's book, *Metaphors in Mind: Transformation through Symbolic Modelling* (2000). What I discovered there was stunningly different from what I had been studying. I ventured into the unknown, following some intuitive hunch (which I highly recommend!), and began my training. When I returned to my work as a school counselor, I was still unsure how applicable Clean Language would be in the "real" world. As if in answer to my doubt, on my first day back a boy walked into my office talking of the "generator in his head" that went to "ultra-boiling" when he had a temper tantrum. As he embellished his description, what emerged was a complex system of sequences, triggers and solutions--fascinating stuff! I was convinced by that nine-year-old that internal metaphors exist for all of us, and I was primed to learn more about how to use them to full advantage to help people heal and grow.

Perhaps you, too, come with a story. You might have heard or read of someone else's experience in a session, and it resonated with you. Ideally, you have had an opportunity to be facilitated in a Clean Language session to discover your own internalized metaphors and come away amazed at what you unearthed. You discovered you could get deeply and quickly to the heart of the matter, to a place you may have had no conscious idea was involved in your issue. Not only could you connect with your inner world, you found you could work with and alter it. That is compelling, indeed!

Or you may be a curious seeker of cutting-edge techniques, and be new to Clean Language and Symbolic Modeling altogether. If so, be prepared to be surprised. You are in for a treat! Most of my first time clients end their session with one of two words, "Wow!" or "Cool!". As you do the exercises in this workbook, you may get glimpses into your own metaphor world. As you work with a practice partner or client, you will discover how you can use this approach to foster significant new insights and promote the possibility of profound helping and healing shifts.

This workbook is written primarily as a training text for students of Symbolic Modeling. It is organized with the idea that its users will be working with partners, alternating roles as facilitator and client. There are also exercises included for those using this for self-directed study, though I would encourage you to do some in-person training, if at all possible; the opportunity to be a client will inform your facilitation immeasurably! Welcome, whatever the story that brings you here and however you choose to learn.

I'd like to offer some words of encouragement for all students of these techniques: hang in there! Be patient as we go through the steps of learning Symbolic Modeling one by one. Learning to facilitate a Symbolic Modeling session is rather like learning to drive. Remember when you first started? If you were anything like me, you couldn't imagine being able to do all the things you have to do at once: accelerate, brake, steer, watch the rear view mirror, watch the cars in front of you, look out for traffic lights, change lanes, and maybe use the clutch and gear shift, and on and on. And you're supposed to figure out where you are going. You've got to be kidding! But once some of those skills became automatic, you could focus on other aspects of driving, and eventually, with lots of practice, it became natural and relatively easy. The same is true of Symbolic Modeling.

I'll be asking you to practice, and it may feel awkward or incomplete until you've got all the questions to work with. Be patient with the process and be patient with yourself. You are learning a new language and, perhaps, a new way of thinking about your role and about your client's wisdom.

The good news is you don't have to try to do all parts of Symbolic Modeling at once to get anywhere, the way you did driving. (Well, you may have started in an empty school parking lot or a country driveway somewhere, but you still had to steer and accelerate and brake, and, and, and...) We will add new Clean Language questions and skills as individually as possible, and, even with only a few, you can have remarkable things happen with clients!

I can tell you with confidence that if you approach the materials here with an open mind and are patient with yourself as you gradually master new skills, you will find this work paradigm-shifting and immensely rewarding. So, find a sense of adventure within and get ready to explore new territory!

Whether you choose to select parts of what you learn here to integrate into your current work or conduct full-on Symbolic Modeling sessions, may what you take from your experience enrich your life and the lives of those you touch.

Gina Campbell
Director and Trainer
Mining Your Metaphors

Contents

About This Book

Before we embark on this journey of discovery and new learning together, take a moment to look over the table of contents. In Part One of this introductory course to Clean Language and Symbolic Modeling, we will be covering nine basic Clean Language questions. (The other three are covered in the next workbook, *Basics Part Two: Facilitating Change*). There are extensive discussions and a plethora of examples to give you not only the whats, but the whys and hows of each of the questions. You will learn how to structure a session from start to finish and to develop facilitation techniques and question-selection strategies. We will emphasize how to guide your clients to explore and strengthen their internal and external resources, things of help or value to them, and how to assist them to get clearer about who they are and what they want. Whatever your helping profession, these skills can be of use to you with your clients.

The workbook is structured to give you opportunities to practice what you're learning each step of the way, with a review at the end of each section. As with any new discipline, you will only get better with practice. The more you practice, the more natural the questions will become, and the more skillfully you will direct your clients' exploration of themselves.

If you are working your way through the book on your own, I encourage you to find a practice partner(s), either someone else learning the process or a client or friend willing to let you practice with them. It's best if you, too, have an opportunity to be a client. The book is divided into seven sections. You might want to browse through the activities in a section before you begin it, so you can arrange to have someone to practice with when it's called for.

Enjoy!

Special note for mental health clinicians: As with any new technique you are learning, you should avoid practicing Symbolic Modeling on fragile clients until you have mastered the skill. This is not to suggest this is not an appropriate technique to use in most cases, but complex information develops very quickly once you delve into metaphor, and one needs to be skilled to manage it. You will most certainly want to study *Basics Part Two: Facilitating Change*, as you will want to have its additional tools and strategies to help your client craft their solutions for problematic blocks and patterns. I suggest particular caution with clients who have difficulty discriminating between reality and fantasy; you need to be a skilled Symbolic Modeling facilitator to take this on.

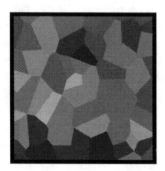

Section One

*"Everywhere I go,
I find that a poet has
been there before me."*

-Sigmund Freud

INTRODUCING SYMBOLIC MODELING

Symbolic Modeling is a language-based, mind/body process that invites your client to achieve greater clarity about any personal topic, including themselves, and to work through problematic issues at a very deep level. The technique can be applied to everyday material that your client accesses consciously. More importantly, it can be applied to symbolic or metaphoric material that emerges from your client's subconscious, material that holds a deeper wisdom and healing potential.

History

Symbolic Modeling is largely based on the pioneering work of counseling psychologist David Grove (1950-2008). In the 1980s, Grove's theories about how people functioned and changed diverged from the NLP (neurolinguistic programming) and Eriksonian hypnosis he had studied. He began to develop innovative techniques that focus on client-generated metaphors to help trauma survivors. His first technique he called **Clean Language**, a progressive questioning technique that uses a client's *exact words* and *internalized metaphors* to clarify personal beliefs, goals and conflicts, and to foster transformative change.

Around the turn of the century, psychotherapists James Lawley and Penny Tompkins systematized Grove's process, adding strategies and refinements that continue to evolve to this day, including the Frameworks for Change and REPROCess model you will learn here. Combining Grove's foundation with insights from cognitive linguistics, systems thinking, and their own research, they call their process **Symbolic Modeling**.

Theory

Clean Language theory regards individuals as mind/body systems whose significant feelings, thoughts, beliefs and experiences are recorded as *internalized metaphors*. Our brains conceive first in these metaphoric images, *then* apply words to those images. Most of the images lie hidden in the subconscious, a subterranean mine of metaphors that influence us without our awareness.

This is why talk alone cannot always access our deepest needs, conflicts, or knowing. What we need is a way to converse with those metaphoric images, to bring their struggles and their wisdom into language so we can hear from them and talk to them. Then we will have input from all the significant parts of the Self: conscious and subconscious, mind and body, assuring that whatever new ideas or solutions we come up with comprehensively address *all* our wants and needs.

Clean Language provides you with a way to establish two-way communication between your client's conscious and subconscious in a language both their conscious and the subconscious understand. Using the five stage Symbolic Modeling process, you can help your client explore their metaphors: their characteristics, organization, interactions and patterns. Frequently, the client discovers self-guiding metaphors whose logic is no longer appropriate. They limit their way of viewing the world, leading to ineffective and/or damaging coping strategies or problematic physical symptoms. Without needing to be interpreted or analyzed, the metaphors will reveal what is working and what is not, what needs to change, and how that change needs to happen. It is this process of discovery and learning that you help your client navigate, trusting that deep within they have all they need to heal and self-regulate to meet the world healthy and whole, emotionally, physically, mentally and spiritually.

By actively engaging your client in determining how their metaphors can change to meet their desired outcomes, transformative shifts can occur within their internalized metaphors. Meaningful changes to thoughts, feelings, and actions follow as new neural pathways are established and strengthened. The old neural pathways don't disappear; the memory is not erased. But new pathways become the go-to routes when a cue, such as a memory or the first step of a pattern, is activated. The client develops a new way of responding which, like the old way, is encoded in metaphor.

Application

While the original applications of Clean Language and Symbolic Modeling were for a therapeutic population and their focus was on metaphor, the techniques are now used by many life and business coaches, as well as body/energy workers, marketing professionals, educators, journalists, and more. The techniques are highly flexible; *it's all about where you as the facilitator direct attention.* This workbook focuses on the application of these skills by helping and healing professionals, such as counselors/therapists and coaches. We will primarily address working with metaphors, though the questions and strategies are exactly the same for everyday material.

The three basic components of Symbolic Modeling

Metaphors: Metaphors are the *content* you work with. These metaphors aren't created the way a client might pick one when writing a poem; instead, they experience them as they already exist in their mind and body, and they are now merely discovering them. Facilitators work with the metaphors as if they are real (for they are, after all, descriptions of what is real!) and refer to them as **internalized** metaphors. The images which make up these metaphors relate to one another, and it is in these relationships that the patterns of your client's behavior, feelings and thoughts are found.

> Metaphors = Content
>
> Clean Language = Tool
>
> Modeling = Strategy

Clean Language: Clean Language is the *tool* you use to work with your client's content. It consists of select words and a special syntax you couple with the client's exact words, to create questions about the symbols/images they describe. These questions guide their attention to the symbols' details and their relationships with one another. You will notice the speech does not sound like ordinary conversation; it is grammatically awkward and very sparse. This encourages the client not to engage cognitively or conversationally with you, as you are there to guide the client's exploration of their metaphors, not to interpret their meanings or add observations.

Modeling: Modeling is the *strategy* you employ to determine what questions to ask to guide your client's attention. You and your client are working on developing a full picture or model of their inner reality. Through a series of questions, and possibly over a number of sessions, you two will collect details about the metaphors with which they have stored their experiences and responses to those experiences.

Think of building a model town for a train set. It is full of objects, laid out to relate to each other in different ways, serving a variety of purposes. You might have a train. It runs on tracks with several curves and may split in places. The tracks go by a number of homes, maybe a bank, and a school house. There may be switch

> Metaphor landscape
>
> Metaphor map
>
> Symbolic domain

controls and lights which regulate the train's going and coming. About each of these, there will be added details and purposes. You could build a miniature model of these that would show these details and interrelationships.

Just so, your client is creating a *model* of their internal metaphors, their internal world. We say they are *self-modeling*, while you are *modeling* with strategically selected Clean Language questions.

We refer to the sum total of a client's images as their **metaphor landscape** and to a drawing or sketch of it as a **metaphor map**—for all of the images are in relation to one another like locations on a map. When the client is connected to this inner world of metaphor, we say they are **in the symbolic domain.** Make a mental note of these three terms, as we will use them often.

Note: We are not using the term modeling to mean role playing, demonstrating, or suggesting how your client should think or behave!

What's a session like for a client?

The answer is, it depends. You can use Clean Language questions and modeling strategies with everyday material, sprinkling them throughout a regular conversation; the client might never be aware you are doing anything special other than helping them discover information extraordinarily effectively. You can even work with client metaphors in a conversational sort of way.

Or you can use the facilitation techniques you will learn here to guide a client into a self-reflective, *mindful*, natural trance state of inner focus that does not feel ordinary. Certainly for counselors and therapists, this is a valuable skill to develop. If you are a coach, you will need to be very mindful of what your contract with your client is. A business coaching client may not be at all interested in being in trance....or they may be fascinated. (I will devote much more time to distinguishing between coaching and counseling in *Basics Part Two*, when we get more deeply into change work.)

What are metaphors?

Before we get started, let's be sure we are clear on how we will be using the word, metaphor. For our purposes, we will be using the term broadly to include similes, analogies, and parables. Definition: a metaphor is a comparison of two unlike things that share one or more qualities or characteristics; a description of one thing or experience in terms of another.

Overt metaphors: These are the ones you're probably most used to identifying.

Examples:

My love is like a *red, red rose*.
Reporters are the *watchdogs* of society.
That exam was a *piece of cake*.
When you fall off a horse, you've got to just get back on.

Embedded metaphors: These often pass by unnoticed. They are *embedded* in our language, part of the very *fabric* of our everyday speech.

Examples:

Did you notice the metaphors implied in the sentences above by the italicized words?

Embodied metaphors: These compare something to an experience in the world as a physical being. They may refer to sensory experiences or how we move in space. As you can see from the examples below, they are often embedded.

Examples:

I have to *push myself* to complete my work.
I want to feel *connected* to my spouse.
I've never gotten *over* his leaving.
I *struggled* with this decision.
When she left me, my world *crumbled around me*.

Gestural metaphors: These embodied metaphors are revealed with body movements.

Examples:

Do you ever put your *hand to your heart* when you speak? What's there?
Ever put y*our hand up and push to the side* when speaking? What's to that side and how far away is it?

1.1 | *Activity*

List several well-known metaphors you can think of:

1.

2.

3.

Why use metaphors?

We Are Natural Metaphor Makers

- Metaphors are fundamental to the way humans think—by comparing. They are found in every language and understood even by the very young. Whether you give attention to your client's metaphors or not, they will be thinking and experiencing metaphorically.

- Metaphors help us communicate efficiently and effectively with one another, particularly when we are trying to describe the intangible. How better to describe it than to compare it to something tangible that it is like in some significant way? Clients often use metaphors to describe feelings.

- Metaphors help us conceptualize and remember what we learn, *whether consciously or subconsciously*. These metaphors, in turn, establish the guidelines we live by, influencing how we react emotionally, what we think, and how we choose to act. Your client's metaphors reveal their interpretations of their experiences and the internal coping strategies they developed in response.

Systems Thinking and Brain Neurology

Clean Language starts with the premise that when the mind/body is challenged to make sense of a new experience, it finds a metaphor for it—something familiar which, for the individual, this new thing is "like." Stored in the subconscious, this metaphor connects to all the same neural pathways as other aspects of that experience, and, possibly, other things that are "like it." Thus, the metaphor becomes part of the neural system of associations.

Since a system functions with feedback, any change or shift in one element of the system can affect change in another element(s). *A change in a metaphor can lead to a change in the Self.* The metaphor does not need to be interpreted or analyzed to have this effect; it is already an interconnected part of the system. Thus, when you work strictly with metaphor, change can happen and healing can occur in other parts of the individual's system. New responses to old stimuli are established in the form of new neural pathways.

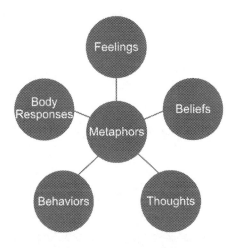

**Change the metaphor, and it impacts the system;
any or all connected parts may shift in response.**

How do you loosen the brain up, encourage it to be receptive to change, when old neural pathways and patterns may have been present for years? Scientists suggest that *experiential* approaches, which connect with the subconscious on emotional and sensory as well as cognitive levels, enhance brain neuroplasticity. With greater plasticity comes a greater capacity for flexibility and change.[1] By actively engaging the mind and body in metaphoric re-imaging, Clean Language works at a deeper level than talk alone.

Safety

Metaphors can offer safety to a client. Their indirect approach to a topic allows the client to deal with what is too shameful or too painful or too frightening to deal with head on. They both *conceal and reveal*. As Emily Dickinson put it, "Tell all the Truth, but tell it slant….The Truth must dazzle gradually/Or every man be blind".[2]

Layers of Meaning

Metaphors can hold a lot of information at once. This is one reason why, in Clean Language, you do not interpret the meaning of the metaphors; they probably mean multiple things. To interpret them might limit the client's ability to address all the meanings in a constructive way that will resolve all that needs resolving before change can stick.

Clients enjoy working with them!

Clients find working with their metaphors absolutely intriguing. They experience their metaphors as meaningful, creative, remarkably somatic or physical, and uniquely personal. As metaphors are expressed both in the mind (usually in words and pictures) and in the body (as feelings, symptoms, and gestures), clients in a Clean Language session feel a sense of experiencing and expressing their complete selves.

1.2	Activity

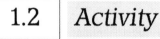

Underline the metaphors in the following sentences. Note: Some will be *overt*, and some will be *implied* or *embedded*.

1. I was under the impression that my contact had set up the interview ahead of time.
2. I found my footing once I went to greater lengths to practice regularly.
3. Now that I'm fully retired, I'm eager to have more time in my life for creative pursuits.
4. Is the whole idea behind this technique to help keep facilitators out of their clients' inner worlds, or to get them in?
5. I strengthened my resolve and made real progress moving forward.
6. Clean Language is a flexible tool, invaluable in any professional's toolbox.
7. The new teacher's quick mind and curiosity energized her students.
8. I carry a ton of responsibility on my back!

Answers start on page 125.

INTRODUCING CLEAN LANGUAGE

The first skill you will be developing is using the tool that its originator, David Grove, called **Clean Language** (the same term he used to describe his methodology, which can be a bit confusing.) It consists of simple questions about what your client says, using their exact words.

This is not about having a conversation. The Clean Language process is a way for you to enable your client to discover more about their inner world. It is a world rich with information, thoughts, feelings, ideas, past history and associations, assumptions, intentions, and strategies for living.

Your role as a facilitator is to listen closely, repeat accurately, and hold the space for your client as you direct their attention. It requires patience and respect to be active as a listener and a questioner while keeping your own opinions and input in reserve. With this client-centered process, you are not there to problem-solve or make change happen. Nevertheless, where you direct your client's attention with the questions you ask is crucial to your client's experience.

> *Facilitator's Role*
> - *Listen closely*
> - *Repeat accurately*
> - *Hold the space*
> - *Direct Attention*

Clean Language is a way to elicit detailed information about what your client currently knows, and this can be helpful. But the chief purpose is to discover new things the client doesn't currently know (or, at least, not consciously.) And surprisingly, with these very simple questions, new and often unexpected information and insights will emerge.

> *Client's Role*
> *Self-exploration*
> *not*
> *Self-examination*

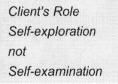

Clean Language, with its own rules of syntax and vocabulary, is distinctive. You may find it sounds awkward; you'll notice it is repetitive. These qualities elegantly serve an intended purpose. They are immediate indications that these are not ordinary questions nor is this an ordinary conversation. Clean Language is an invitation to *self-exploration*, not a vehicle for *self-explanation* (though it may accomplish that, too.)

While you may certainly end up deciding that the full Clean Language syntax is not what you will choose to use in every situation or conversation with your clients, for now you'll be learning and practicing Clean Language in its 'pure state.' This way, you can experience the difference doing so makes and be able to make an informed choice as to when to use it.

Clean Language Syntax

What we call a Clean Language question (**CLQ**) actually consists of a statement(s) and a question. In what we call full syntax, it has three parts. As I said before, it doesn't sound like ordinary speech, nor will the sentence always sound grammatically logical. Nonetheless, there are good reasons to stick to its wording precisely. A typical Clean Language question sounds like this:

Examples:

Client: *It's taken awhile, but I feel like I'm finally on solid ground.*

Facilitator: And feel like you're finally on solid ground.
                 And when on solid ground, what kind of solid is that solid?

Thus, the format of a Clean Language question looks like this.

Facilitator: **And** [all or selected parts of client's statement]
                 And when [repeats selected part of client's statement],
                 [**Clean Language question**]?

FAQ | Frequently Asked Questions

Clean Language sounds like it would be so wooden and stilted. How could a client feel really connected with me, much less get much out of a session?

If you're new to Clean Language and Symbolic Modeling and are wondering what a session sounds like or how this could be effective, you can register for a Free Introduction to Clean Language webinar at https://app.ruzuku.com/courses/32779/about Go to Clean Language in Action. You will discover that, in fact, facilitating with Clean Language sounds remarkably natural and gets to core issues very quickly. As for connection, when you repeat your client's exact words, they sense your engagement.

Why is it called Clean Language?

It is called *clean* because the facilitator works to keep their own word choices and assumptions to a minimum so as not to contaminate or influence the client's metaphor landscape. No word choice is arbitrary or neutral, and a facilitator can't possibly know what meaning or resonance a particular word might have for a client. Therefore remaining clean, sticking precisely with the client's words, means you will most surely be working with the client's world view and their understanding of it.

Why start every statement with "And..."?

You will notice that starting with "And..." gives your sentence a rhythmic, hypnotic quality. Clean Language is very much about rhythm. (In fact, David Grove studied Shakespeare and poet Dylan Thomas while determining the exact phrasing to use.) Clients wholly immersed in their metaphor landscapes are often in a deeply mindful, inner-focused or natural trance state, and using "And..." encourages them to remain in it. Everything I've heard and seen with clients suggests that this is the state in which they are in communication with their subconscious minds.

"And..." also suggests that your client's repeated words and your questions are a natural continuation of their thoughts from their perspective. This encourages your client to stay in that inner-focused state and exploration process and not to engage in conversation with you.

Why do you repeat the client's words more than once?

By repeating the client's statement once, you *acknowledge* to the client that you've truly heard them. The repetition also slows them down, giving them time to notice the information/image(s), to take in more details, and to experience the accompanying feelings.

Your second repetition begins to *narrow the scope* of the client's attention, allowing still more time for all the above.

Then your question *focuses their attention* on a particular area of or detail in their metaphor landscape.

> • *Acknowledge*
> • *Narrow scope*
> • *Focus attention*

It is as if you are (1) panning a camera around the scene the client has described, (2) zooming in on a smaller section of the whole, and (3) bringing the lens into even clearer focus on a detail.

The repetition, like the "And...", is hypnotically soothing and trance-inducing, further encouraging a mindful inner-focused state. It also helps the client (and you!) remember all the landscape as it continues to emerge.

Do I have to use all three parts of the Clean Language question every time?

For now, yes. You need the practice. Once you get really good at using all three parts, we will discuss when you might leave out the first and/or second repetition, or even add another repetition after the question. This is not done randomly, but for deliberate effect.

How effective could this really be? Isn't my client paying me for my expertise?

It's a rare experience for a client coming to a helping professional to have a substantial amount of time and space to explore their inner reality uninterrupted. The professional will usually attempt to problem solve, make some change happen, or otherwise offer direction, give advice and/or make a plan. While using Symbolic Modeling may not be appropriate for *every* situation, I think you'll be surprised to discover how often, when aided in this open-ended way, people are capable of devising a way to help and/or heal themselves—*despite* what their current choices of behavior might suggest. I have had trainees in the past who have struggled mightily to let go of their normal way of controlling a session. When they open up to the Symbolic Modeling process, they come to be profoundly moved by what emerges. Try trusting the process and trusting your client's inner wisdom as you learn Symbolic Modeling, and see what happens.

Clean Language Overview

Its purpose:
- to assist the client in self-modeling, i.e. developing a full picture of their metaphor landscape
- to access the client's inner, subconscious wisdom
- to assure the client's content remains free of the facilitator's personal content

Its elements:
- client's precise words
- specific, simply-worded questions
- special syntax

Its benefits:
- helps keep the facilitator's assumptions out of the process
- helps client model their inner world accurately
- maintains emphasis on client self-exploration rather than self-explanation
- enhances the facilitator's empathetic connection with the client

It helps a client:
- feel listened to, respected
- feel in control over what they reveal
- feel empowered
  - the client's answers come from within, independent from the facilitator
  - the client takes responsibility for their own healing
  - the client sets the pace
- practice tuning into their intuitive wisdom
- experience the significance and power of the vocabulary of their self-talk and of their intentions

MODELING YOUR CLIENT'S INNER REALITY

You can select Clean Language questions to focus your client's attention on many different details and aspects of their metaphor landscape as it emerges. You will make choices on what to ask about based on your client's wants and what you will learn in this workbook about Symbolic Modeling strategies. To begin learning how to effectively develop a model of your client's inner world, we will use part of the acronym REPROCess, as conceived by Lawley and Tompkins, to help you remember some of the key things to be thinking about.

But first, consider the entire word *reprocess*. In a sense, reprocessing is what you will often be doing with clients. You will be helping them discover their current way of processing information and experiences. And, if the resulting feelings or thoughts or actions are not what they want, you will be helping them develop a new process that suits them and their needs better. The clients will be "re-processing" their own systems.

As for our acronym, REPROCess:

R stands for Resources. Resources are valuable or helpful to the individual identifying them. They can come from other people, from the natural world, or from man-made objects. Resources can also be internal. They include knowledge and skills and, particularly significant for us to recognize here, they can be *valuable, helpful states of being or feeling*. Clients can also have resourceful metaphors or symbols in their metaphor landscapes.

E stands for Explanations. Clients are often eager to fill you in on their past histories or to analyze or otherwise explain their feelings, actions, etc. You want to avoid getting sucked into these explanations, because, to a significant degree, the problem now lies not in the past, but in the way clients have structured their beliefs and strategies about how best to manage being in the world in the present.

PRO stands for Problem/Remedy/Outcome. This is a fundamental strategy for determining where to focus a client's attention. P/R/O is at the heart of Symbolic Modeling.

C stands for Change. In this *Basics Part One* workbook, we will be emphasizing how to help a client get clearer about issues, feelings, desires, etc. Greater clarity is a change in and of itself. Often, like dominoes falling, it may be all a client needs for changes in other thoughts, feelings, and behaviors to follow. But when clarity alone doesn't suffice in helping a client achieve their wants or needs, there are other strategies we can employ. *Basics Part Two* will address these.

And the *ess*? Well, it's just there as part of reprocess, not the acronym. Not very neat, but if you find it helpful to remember REPROCess, then we can settle for good enough.

With these handy letters in mind, I am able to quickly categorize "What kind of information am I hearing?", which helps me select which line of questioning to pursue next.

Section One Summary

A client's Symbolic Modeling Session is a process of discovery and change that you as a facilitator help them navigate, trusting that they have all the wisdom they need to heal themselves and meet the world healthy and whole.

The **brain's neuroplasticity**, its capacity to change, is activated by experiential processes like Symbolic Modeling that engage the subconscious.

Symbolic Modeling has three parts:
* **Metaphors** and the **content** you work with
* **Clean Language** is the **tool** you use
* **Modeling** is the **strategy** you employ so your client's metaphor landscape emerges.

Metaphors can be over, embedded, embodies, and gestural. A **metaphor map** is a drawing or other representation of the symbols in a **client's metaphor landscape.**

Change the metaphor, and other aspects of the client's system change too, because the metaphor is an integral part of that system.

Among the **benefits** of **Clean Language** is that the facilitator's own word choices and assumptions are held in check, allowing an accurate picture of the client's inner world to emerge. Clients are empowered as experts on themselves and developers of their own solutions. **Clean Language** is **clean** because the facilitator repeats the client's words accurately, with no added words of their own other than the simple CL questions.

REPROCess stands for:
> **R**esource
> **E**xplanation
> **P**roblem
> **R**emedy
> **O**utcome
> **C**hange
> and **-ess** is there to remind you to thing of reprocessing itself!

My take-away from this section is...

Questions I have...

1.3 Review Activity

Clients don't usually give you simple, one line statements. Underline the metaphors in these longer ones.

1. Every night when it's time for homework, there's a battle with my boys. If they're not arguing with me, they're arguing with each other. It's like it's a contest to get my attention, and once they have it, all they want to do is complain. They really push my buttons, and I'm at my wit's end!

2. I went to college thinking I was going to pursue a degree in math, but I've done an about-turn, and my father's not happy with me. I discovered I am really drawn to theatre, and he's sure I'll be a pauper the rest of my life. He's threatening to cut me off, not pay my tuition. I don't want to be left high and dry or saddled with a boatload of loans! I'm not sure how to approach him now.

3. I've been working under bosses all my life. I want to strike out on my own! I know it's a gamble and it'll be a lot of hard work, but I want to open an Internet cafe in my town. You know, sort of a neighborhood watering hole, like on that old TV show Cheers, but without the beer.

4. Playing sports has always been a huge part of my life, and being an athlete is a big part of my identity. I've always felt people saw me as larger than life, you know? And that gave me confidence. But now... with this injury..., that's all going to change. I'm not that person anymore. Who am I now? Where do I fit in?

Answers start on page 125.

Section Two

"We inhabit a deeply imagined world that exists alongside a real one. Even the crudest utterance, or the simplest, contains the fundamental poetry by which we live."

–Diane Ackerman

Now that you have an overall idea of what Symbolic Modeling and Clean Language are and a general idea of some strategies to guide you as to which details to ask questions about to model a metaphor landscape, let's begin learning the most basic Clean Language questions by applying them to the *R* in REPROCess, Resources.

IDENTIFYING RESOURCES

A resource is something that the client identifies as being helpful or valuable to them in some way. You can often identify a potential resource by noticing when a client identifies a *feeling* or *state of being* that, once achieved, will allow them to do what they want to do or change what they need to change. We refer to these as **resource states**.

Examples:

Client: *I want to be calm and focused when I talk with my teenager.*
Client: *I want to feel centered and relaxed when I meet with my boss about a promotion.*

Here are some examples from my clients' sessions of states they identified as resourceful:

Accepting	At one with	Balanced	Calm	Centered
Clear	Confident	Connected	Courage	Creative
Empowered	Energetic	Excited	Focused	Free
Grounded	In the flow	Joyful	Knowing	Loving
Mindful	Motivated	Open	Playful	Powerful
Relaxed	Safe	Strong	Trusting	Worthy

It's not that these states are always going to be resourceful. Always consider the context the client provides for these words. For a word to represent a resource, the client needs to make clear this is something they value. To be **open** in a safe context might be desirable; in another context, it could leave a person vulnerable to harm. *Resources are always about context and the individual.*

At other times, as a client develops a landscape, symbols will appear which behave in some way to help the client. These, too, are a type of resource. We call these **resource symbols**.

Examples:

*   My confidence is *a tree trunk* that runs along my spine.

*   I have *a pair of scissors* in my knapsack to cut the ties that bind me.

*   There's *a guard* who takes over the watch so I can rest.

Be on the lookout for both types of potential resources. Once you have verified that they are resources, that they are something your client considers of value, use your CLQs to enable your client to get more familiar with them. And keep track of the resources and their details in your notes, for your client will likely refer to them again.

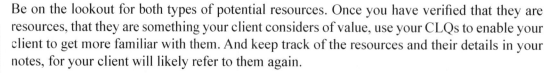

When you help a client develop a new resource or strengthen an existing one, they will meet their problems in a new way, with new coping tools. This includes the metaphoric ones. Who knows what those scissors stand for in the client's inner world? When you work in the world of metaphor, you need to become comfortable with not knowing, and trust your client and the process. Both will surprise you.

Make no assumptions: what can seem like a threat or a problem symbol can become a resource! A monster that frightens a client one moment might use its strength and fierceness to protect them the next. So what happens if you end up helping a client make a change that eliminates such a monster? As long as you remain neutral and make no assumptions about what the client wants to have happen, you will not inadvertently "get rid of" a potential resource symbol. I have noticed clients don't destroy them, even if they don't know why at the time.

CLEAN LANGUAGE QUESTIONS

Symbolic Modeling uses 12 basic Clean Language questions to elicit information, whether you are asking about real life or metaphors. *Basics Part One* will cover nine of them. We will begin with two that you use over and over and over again—that help *develop* key details about the symbols in your client's metaphor landscape, including resources. Hence, we call them *developing* questions.

Clean Language Questions #1 and #2: Attributes

Client: [*statement: xy*]

Facilitator: "And [xy].
                 And when [x],
                 is there anything else about that [x]?"

                 "And [xy].
                 And when [x],
                 what kind of [x] is that [x]?"

These two questions are the most frequently used throughout a Symbolic Modeling session. Don't let their simplicity fool you into thinking you can be careless about their exact wording. The open-ended nature and the rhythm of the words, just the way they are, is important. The exact repetition of questions said exactly the same way is important: it means the client does not have to give much thought to what you are asking of their information and can focus instead on their answer and the feelings that accompany it.

Here is an example of the attribute questions being used in a session where the client is already deeply into their symbolic domain or metaphor landscape.

Example:

Client:	*I'm walking down a path, and it's sunny out.*
Facilitator:	And walking down a path and sunny. And when walking down a path, what kind of path is that path?
Client:	*It's fairly wide, wider than I need.*
Facilitator:	And fairly wide, wider than you need. And when walking down a path wider than you need, is there anything else about that wider?
Client:	*Yes, I just realized, I'm not alone. There're two people with me, two girls...I think they're my old high school friends.*
Facilitator:	And not alone and two girls. And when two girls, is there anything else about that two?
Client:	*The thought just occurred to me, twice as nice. It's twice as nice, and I'm not alone.*
Facilitator:	And twice as nice. And when twice as nice, what kind of nice is that nice?

Notice when you are repeating, you don't need to repeat every word—just enough to recall the images for the client. Notice, too, how leaving out some of the words makes your sentences less conversational, more trance-inducing.

You can ask about any word. It's natural at first to concentrate on the nouns and adjectives, and they are important, but often you can get some surprising information from a less obvious word. Practice asking questions of them all!

Practicing Attribute Questions about Resources

One of the first places you can begin directing a client's attention is to their resources, both resource states and resource symbols, so they can get to know them better. Just by doing so, the client often strengthens them.

The same can be said for problem states and symbols, which is why you **don't** want to be putting your client's attention on problems. Why strengthen them? Take a moment now to really sit with this last concept, because most of us have been well-trained to focus on problems, to problem-solve. More about this later, but for now, remember to be listening for **resource words**. Focus your client's attention on strengths or what they have identified as needing to strengthen or have more of.

Help clients get to know their resource states and resource symbols better.

2.1 | *Activity*

Begin by reading each statement and identifying resources. Ask yourself: What is of *value* to the client? Then practice asking questions of resource words or phrases in the sentences. I suggest you write and say aloud your Clean Language questions. Your body/brain uses all your senses to learn! Here's the Clean Language syntax again:

Client: *For me, serving others is an important value.*

Clean Language Questions (CLQs):

Facilitator: "And [serving others is an important value].
  And when [serving],
  is there anything else about that [serving]? Or
  what kind of [serving] **is that** [serving]?"

1. I am very efficient at running meetings.

2. I want to balance my work and play.

3. I feel a ball of energy in my gut that starts glowing when I get on the court.

4. I'd like to access the feeling that everything I need is already there waiting for me.

5. I want my success to flow naturally and easily.

6. My professor is so welcoming of our ideas. It gives me the confidence to speak up in class.

7. If I push myself harder, I'm sure I can win his trust.

Answers on page 126.

2.2 | Activity

Choose a resource state you would like to have more of. Practice with the first two Clean Language attribute questions by using them to explore yourself. I'll give you an example to get you started, keeping the client's answers deliberately short. If you're working with a partner, I encourage you both to keep your answers short when you are the client as well, as it takes a lot of practice as a facilitator to be able to repeat back information, and this is only your first go at it.

Example:

Client: *I want to be more open.*

Facilitator: And you want to be more open. And when open, what kind of open is that open?

Client: *It's natural, like that's the way it's meant to be.*

Facilitator: And natural, that's the way it's meant to be. And when open is natural and the way it's meant to be, is there anything else about open?

Client: *It's easy, relaxed.*

Facilitator: And relaxed, easy. And when easy, what kind of easy is that easy?

Client: *Yeah, I like it!*

Facilitator: And you like it! And is there anything else about that easy?

Client: It's easy to choose not to be open, too.

Your client's answers may not correspond to the question you asked exactly or be the sort of answer you were expecting. The point is not to satisfy you, the facilitator, but to help the client explore. As long as the client is getting more useful information, that's okay. Trust the client's inner wisdom; what's coming up is just what they need to know.

Your turn now. Use the resource state you selected to answer the following questions. If your resource state had more than one word in it, (ex. I want to be calm and relaxed.), pick *one word* at a time to explore, just as you should do with a client.

Resource #1: _____

1. And what kind of [#1] is that [#1]?

2. And is there anything else about that [#1]?

Now choose another word from one of your answers above to explore:

3. And what kind of [word] is that [word]?

4. And is there anything else about that [word]?

Clean Language Question #3: Invitation to Metaphor

You will be doing a lot of work with your client's metaphors, for reasons you are now familiar with. Some clients move naturally into metaphors, but there will be other times when you will need to invite your client to move into metaphor (and not just near the beginning of a session.) When you do, the Clean Language question is:

"And that's [x]... like... what?"

As you might have guessed by now, resource words are the ones to be asking about, as they will be helpful for your client to call upon as needed. Often they suggest a visual image when you hear them, such as "open" in the example below. But some individuals would describe them as being auditory, tactile, kinesthetic and so on. You need to develop a very keen ear for those implied, embedded metaphors, the ones that easily *slip* by!

Example:

Facilitator: And you want to be **open**, natural, easy, relaxed. And you can choose...
And when **open**,
that's **open** like what?

Client: *It's **open** like a book.*

Once you have a metaphor for the resource, you explore it the same way you did the original resource word, with Clean Language attribute questions.

Example continued:

Facilitator: And open like a book. And when a book, what kind of book is that book?

Client: *It's large, it's got a red cover... leather, I think.*

Facilitator: And leather, red cover, large. And is there anything else about that open book?

Client: *I know I'm the one who opens it, and I can close it if I want to.*

Facilitator: And you open it, and you can close it if you want to. And when want to, what kind of want is that want?

Client: *When it's someone I trust and want to be close, I open the book. When I don't want to connect with the person, I can shut it or leave it closed.*

Facilitator: And someone you trust and want to be close to. And what kind of someone is that someone?

Client: *I see a child in front of me, and I want to read the child a story from the book.*

Surprised? You may have been expecting more details about the book or about feelings associated with the book, but what emerged were two new symbols: a child and a story. That's how a metaphor landscape unfolds sometimes!

Notice in the last question I asked, when the information really starts flowing, I didn't use all three parts of the full syntax. I encourage you to practice with all three parts for now, until your choice to *not* do so is an informed one. Besides, you'll find that the repetition not only serves your client, it serves you. It may not be happening for you yet, but eventually, remembering what your client says comes more naturally. You can then use the time spent on repeating to decide what question you're going to ask! Can't imagine multi-tasking like that? Remember when you first started driving...?

2.3 | *Activity*

Referring back to your last activity, you have gotten some information about the attributes and characteristics of your Resource #1. If a metaphor has not emerged for you yet (which is fine), you can "take it into metaphor," as we say, by asking the simple Clean Language question: **"And that's [x] like what?"** You can do this exercise with a partner, or, if you're on your own, write out your full question here (It should have three parts!), then switch hats to become the client and answer it.

And (phrase about your resource) _____,
And when (narrow focus towards resource) _____,
that's (resource word) _____ like what?

Answer with words and a drawing. (No drawing talent necessary. Stick figures are fine. Park you inner critic at the door, to use a helpful metaphor!)

Now develop some information about your metaphor.

1. And what kind of [#1metaphor] is that [#1metaphor]?

2. And is there anything else about that [#1metaphor]?

Now choose a word from one of your answers above to explore:

3. And what kind of [word] is that [word]?

4. And is there anything else about that [word]?

You see how you could keep developing more and more information with these simple questions? So, keep going! Keep asking these basic Clean Language questions of the words that emerge for you. Add the new information to the drawing, as it emerges.

Choose two more resource words, and repeat the process with your other two resource words. It will be interesting to discover if the process feels similar for you each time or different, given your different resourceful states.

Resource #2: _____

1. And what kind of [#2] is that [#2]?

2. And is there anything else about that [#2]?

Now choose a word from one of your answers above to explore:

3. And what kind of [word] is that [word]?

4. And is there anything else about that [word]?

If a metaphor has not yet emerged, take your #2 resource word and take it into metaphor by asking, "**And that's [x] like what?**" Write out your full question here, then answer it.

And _____

And when _____,

that's _____ **like what?**

Answer with words and a drawing. (Remember, park you inner critic at the door!)

Now develop some information about your metaphor.

1. And what kind of [#2 metaphor] is that [#2 metaphor]?

2. And is there anything else about that [#2 metaphor]?

Choose a word from one of your answers above to explore:

3. And what kind of [word] is that [word]?

4. And is there anything else about that [word]?

Anything you want to add to your drawing, your metaphor map? Go right ahead!

Resource #3: _____

1. And what kind of [#2] is that [#2]?

2. And is there anything else about that [#2]?

Now choose a word from one of your answers above to explore:

3. And what kind of [word] is that [word]?

4. And is there anything else about that [word]?

If a metaphor has not yet emerged for your #3 resource word, take it into metaphor by asking, **"And that's [x] like what?"** Write out you full question here, and answer it.

And _____

And when _____,

that's _____ **like what?**

Answer with words and a drawing.

Now develop some information about your answer.

1. And what kind of [#3 metaphor] is that [#3 metaphor]

2. ?And is there anything else about that [#3 metaphor]?

Now choose a word from one of your answers above to explore:

3. And what kind of [word] is that [word]?

4. And is there anything else about that [word]?

By now, you know to return to your drawing, your metaphor map, and add any new details you'd like to add. Sometimes just doing this leads to still more discoveries.

Note: We have been practicing with inner resourceful states, but these aren't the only kinds of resources you can develop. More on that to come.

You are ready now to practice developing a resource with your three Clean Language questions with a practice buddy or client. Not sure you can? Let me address one concern people new to Symbolic Modeling often have.

What if I take a long time to come up with a question?

Silence is your friend. One of the advantages of live training, when you get to be a client, too, is that you will quickly realize that more is going on for the client than the facilitator hears about. Once your client is deeply immersed in their symbolic domain or metaphor world, they are unlikely to even notice that you are taking what seems to you like a long time. So, don't worry about it! Besides, you're a novice here; let your client know you are learning a new skill, and take all the time you need.

A Classic Slip-Up

Careful not to ask your client for a metaphor of a metaphor. What do I mean?

Example:

Client: *I've come to a fork in the road. Deciding which way to go is tearing me apart!*

Facilitator: And a fork in the road. And deciding is tearing you apart. And when a fork in the road, that's a fork in the road like what?

Don't think you'd ever do that? Well, it happens. You are just concentrating so hard on so many things when you are first learning. If you do make such a mistake, your client is likely to just repeat the same information. Pick it up from there. Don't distract your client with apologies or mumbling, "What was I thinking!"

Example continued:

Client: *Uh....like a fork in the road!?*

Facilitator: And a fork in the road. And when a fork, is there anything else about that fork?

2.4 | *Activity*

Partner practice. Begin by asking your buddy/client to identify a feeling they want more of in life. (Presumably this is a resource.) Spend about 10 minutes on each session.

You can keep this chart open in front of you to remind yourself of the questions. Plan on spending 6-8 minutes per session.

CLQs: **"And what kind of [x] is that [x]?"**

"And is there anything else about that [x]?"

"And that's [x] like... what?"

Afterwards, answer the following questions:

Something I did well was:

Something I want to work on next time is:

Section Two Summary

Resources are things that have value to the client because they are helpful in some way. They may be both **personal qualities or characteristics (resource states)** and **symbolic metaphors (resource symbols).**

When you help a client learn more about a new resource or strengthen an existing one, they will meet their problems in a new way, with new coping tools and strategies. One way to do this is to find and develop a **metaphor for a resource state.**

My take-away from this section is...

Questions I have...

2.5 | *Review Activity*

Listen for the implied metaphors embedded in the following sentences. Using full, three-part Clean Language syntax, practice asking for a metaphor. If you're working with a partner, the client will answer once, and the facilitator will ask a follow-up attribute question. If you're working alone, alternate being the facilitator and the client, *write* out the questions and answers, and ask your questions *aloud*!

CLQ: **"And that's [x] like what?"**

Example:

Client: *I need to pull myself together.*

Facilitator: And need to pull yourself together. And when pull yourself together, that's pull yourself together like what?

Client: *Like I'm sewing two pieces of fabric together with a needle and thread.*

Facilitator: And sewing two pieces of fabric, and needle and thread. And when needle and thread, is there anything else about that thread?

1. I want to be at the top of the top of the class.

2. I'm really drawn to more exploring of possible new renewable energy sources.

3. I want to go easy on myself when I am learning something new.

4. As I picture my future now, it's full steam ahead.

5. We're working towards reconciliation.

6. I want to make a solid commitment to our life together.

7. I'm wondering how I can be playful even when I am working.

8. I want to get my temper under my control.

9. When I get home from work, I want to leave it behind and be fully present for my family.

10. I would like to be able to stand up to my grandfather when he bullies my mother.

Answers on page 126.

Section Three

"When someone deeply listens to you
your bare feet are on the earth
and a beloved land that seemed
distant is now at home within you."

–John Fox

FACILITATING A SESSION FROM START TO FINISH

You could close this book right now, and have some very useful tools:
- three Clean Language questions
- a whole new understanding of metaphors
- an idea of how to develop a resource

And you've only just begun to tap into the rich potential of mining your client's metaphors with the systematic process! But I don't want you to have to wait until we cover it all before you begin applying to your client sessions what you've learned. Section Three will give you and overview of how to conduct a Symbolic Modeling session from start to finish. You'll then have a basic framework to build on as we continue to add more questions and strategies.

It starts with situating

A session begins when the client enters to the room and you ask two questions:

> **"And where would you like to be?"** (notice, the word is not *sit*, but *be*.)

and, once the client is settled,

> **"And where would you like me to be?"**

Obviously, the dictates of your space may not allow for much flexibility, but when possible, let the client choose their space. Encourage them to adjust the angle of their seat, your seat, their distance apart, any aspect you are able to put in their control. Let them experiment. Even after you sit down, check in again, "Is this alright?"

This signals several things to the client:

- You are not in a traditional authoritative, in-control position, which helps set the stage for a session where the client is the one determining their desired outcome.

- The client is being directed to take some responsibility for the session. Theirs is not going to be a passive role.

Also, the client tunes in to their intuitive knowing to assess their response to the space, a sensitivity they will benefit from enhancing.

Clients may not realize it because they've never been given the choice before, but there's probably a set-up that best enables them to concentrate and open up. So, don't take, "Oh, whatever you want is fine!" If they need a prompt, let them experiment with trying different possibilities. Sit right in front of the client, then sit perpendicular to them. Which do they prefer? Does the distance apart make a difference?

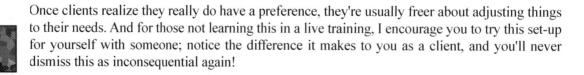

Once clients realize they really do have a preference, they're usually freer about adjusting things to their needs. And for those not learning this in a live training, I encourage you to try this set-up for yourself with someone; notice the difference it makes to you as a client, and you'll never dismiss this as inconsequential again!

So, once you're both settled, then what? You may have your own way of starting with a client, including assessing the first time client or getting filled in on what's happened since your last session. What we're addressing here is how to start the *Symbolic Modeling* session, whether it is all or a part of what you do with your client.

We are going to jump some letters in our REPROCess acronym now, and focus on the *O*.

Clean Language Question #4: Establishing A Desired Outcome

O is for outcome, Desired Outcome, to be more precise. The question that begins every session, and which comes up again and again during a session, is simple, but can be surprisingly profound:

> **"And what would you like to have happen?"**

The question is about intention, as it directs the client to focus attention on what they *want*, not on the problem they have. Guiding your client's attention to develop a detailed picture of their outcome will strengthen it, rather than reinforcing the problem state they find themselves in. We will work with problems more when we get to the problem/remedy/outcome of REPROCess, but you can start now beginning your sessions with this question.

What if your practice partner starts talking about something they *don't want*? This might well happen, as we are well-trained at examining our problems. Repeat what they said (acknowledge), and focus your attribute question on something positive they have already mentioned (leaving aside the problem). If their response is only about the problem, go back to this first question: "And what would you like to have happen?"

Example:

Facilitator: And what would you like to have happen?

Client: *I want to have more confidence.*

Facilitator: And you want to have more confidence.
And when more confidence,
what kind of confidence is that confidence?

Client: *The confidence to speak my mind. When I was growing up, my father always criticized me. He shot down any opinion I offered, so now I get nervous when I have an idea.*

So what do you ask about? Don't get drawn into the explanation. Don't ask about nervous; don't ask about the critical father. You can acknowledge such things in your first repeat, but don't develop lots of information about them. (Why dig those neural pathways any deeper?) Go back to the confidence they want more of or ask the first question again. When you get more skilled, you'll learn how to work with the problem; sometimes it can't be set aside. But if you develop a fuller picture of the client's desired outcome first, they come back to the problem with a more resourceful perspective.

Facilitator: And nervous. And shot down. And confidence to speak your mind. And when confidence to speak your mind, is there anything else about that confidence?

Notice that your starting question evoked something desirable, in this case a resource. That's a **Desired Outcome**.

• It is a want, desire, or need for something new or more of something they have

• It projects in to the future

• Client makes no reference to a problem

3.1 | *Activity*

Underline the desired outcomes in the following sentences.

Example:

Facilitator: And what would you like to have happen?

Client: *I want to be <u>able</u> to <u>freely speak my mind</u>.*

1.   I want to feel confident about my decisions.

2.   I want my energy to flow freely and evenly.

3.   I want to be able to think about the future in a more hopeful way.

4.   I wish I could hold onto an insight and run with it.

5.   I need to find a new source of motivation.

6.   I would like a better work-life balance.

7.   I'd love to be comfortable in my own skin!

8.   I want to convey to my clients that I really care about their problems.

Answers start on page 125.

To encourage my clients to think in terms of desired outcomes, I ask them to fill out this next form, and scan and email it, or take a picture and text it to me before the session or simply bring it with them. Clients often tell me they spend a lot of time thinking about this seemingly simple question.

You'll notice the Before Our Session sheet asks for a drawing, as well as a verbal answer. This is another way to invite a client into metaphor—for having to put thoughts or words into pictures requires using symbols of some sort. I begin the session, then, by having the client repeat or read aloud their written desired outcome, making any changes or additions they feel inspired to make and/or describe their drawings. This gives us lots of 'exact words' to get started with.

Before Our Session

To begin our session, consider this question. Feel free to write as little or as much as you like.

What would you like to have happen?

In the space below or on another sheet of paper, do a drawing of what this issue is like for you now and a second drawing of what you would like it to be like. NO artistic talent is required here; stick figures are fine.

Concept by Penny Tompkins and James Lawley

FACILITATING TECHNIQUES

The way your Clean Language question is delivered is almost as important as the words themselves. It's something you will work on in an in-depth live training. If you're on your own, be sure to seek out an opportunity to listen to an experienced facilitator. (To watch a live session, you can register for a Free Introduction to Clean Language webinar at https://app.ruzuku.com/courses/32779/about Go to Clean Language in Action.)

The techniques described here are intended to induce a natural trance-like state of mindful inner focus, appropriate for a private session. It is in an altered state that the client will have easier access to the deeper mind/body wisdom of the subconscious. If you are working in a different sort of context (ex. a classroom, a courtroom, or a boardroom), a trance state would not be appropriate, and so you would want to modify your facilitation to fit the circumstances.

Voice and Pacing

In general, slow down. One of your roles as facilitator is to slow down your client's experience of their landscape, so they can notice and experience more. Remember the panning camera? (See page 11.) Your calm, steady, slow voice helps create a safe space. Your slower pace, along with your "awkward" syntax, is less like normal conversation, encouraging your client to stay in the symbolic domain rather than try to converse with you.

Match your Client: If your client slows down, slow down more; if they speed up, speed up somewhat, too. Match tone and word emphasis. This helps a client hear themselves again, in a sense, and feel truly heard and empathized with.

Keep neutral: Aim for a calm, neutral facial expression. Don't show surprise unless your client has expressed surprise. Don't show pleasure or displeasure, as it may imply to your client that they have given a right or wrong answer. Remember: no assumptions. You'll be surprised how a client's comment or symbol that seems like a "positive" can suddenly become a "negative" and vice versa, and suddenly your response will have been inappropriate. And you don't want your client to get off track by trying to seek your approval or take care of your feelings.

Mirroring: Having encouraged you to remain neutral, there are times when you will want to mirror your client's response. For example, if your client laughs, it may seem natural to laugh, too; it could, at times, be artificial and even ridiculous if you were to sit there, stony-faced, while your client laughed. But I suggest you aim to smile or laugh slightly less than your client, keeping your empathetic connection, but preparing for a shift, too.

Take your time: Silence is your friend. When you don't know what to say next, try being quiet. See what the client notices. I'll give you a sneak preview: if there's been a long pause, you can ask what we call a specialized Clean Language question,

"And what's happening?"

Non-verbals

Be aware of gestures, the direction of your client's gaze, sounds (like sighs or uh-ohs), facial expressions and other non-verbals that might hold information related to your client's metaphor landscape. All gestures are metaphoric in nature, except for actually pointing to a place to locate a particular space or direction. Now, obviously you can't ask about every gesture; but if your client is talking, for example, about some repeating pattern and makes a spiraling motion with their hand, likely that hand is gesturing about some metaphor of which they may not yet be consciously aware; maybe it's a hamster wheel or a race track. That would be a good gesture to ask about.

When referring to a non-verbal of any sort, don't label it with a word of your own. Refer to it by gesturing in the same direction or same place to which the client gestured, or by making the same gesture, and ask the client: "What kind of [make the gesture] is that?" or "Is there anything else about [gesture]?" or "And is there anything else about [looking and gesturing in the direction the client pointed to]?"

The direction in which a client is looking or gesturing may be a clue as to the location of a symbol for which you already have attributes, or it may suggest a new symbol that hasn't been verbalized yet and may not be in the client's conscious awareness. You may choose to ask about it. When? Well, if your client always looks out the window to think, perhaps it's not significant. But if the same client suddenly starts looking up into a corner of the room in an oddly concentrated way, check it out. Be curious: if you have an intuitive hunch that something's different, that you're suddenly aware of where the client is looking, gesture to your client's reference point; don't gesture on your body.

> *Gesture towards your client's reference point.*

Example:

Client: *"It's in my heart. (and lays their hand on their chest)"*

Facilitator: "And it's in your heart (gestures towards client's chest.) And when your heart, what kind of heart is that heart... (gestures towards client's chest again)?"

Notice I say gesture towards, not point at. Pointing can feel intrusive, especially when done towards a woman's chest or anyone's belly area, near the groin. In the example, I mention gesturing twice. That's because any gesture to the chest and any direct looking at that area, I make very brief. Both help direct energy and focus to this area, but with so many people having had sexual abuse issues (and you may never know), I encourage you to be careful and respectful.

Facial expressions are vital clues for the timing of your questions. Notice when a client is thinking, processing or experiencing more. From your own experience as a client, you probably know a lot more is going on for them than you are hearing about, so be patient and let that happen. Look for clues that your client has finished processing your last question and the information there has emerged before asking another question. Don't feel you have to fill the silences.

Watch your own hands! If you're like me, you gesticulate a lot with your hands when you talk. But as you point and wave your hands around, you are intruding on your client's metaphor landscape, your gestures subtly suggesting directions and locations, even other metaphors. Figure out a way to keep your hands still; perhaps holding a pen in one hand and your notepad's top with the other will help.

Eye Contact

Generally, keep minimal eye contact. This helps keep the client from approaching the facilitation process like a conversation, checking for your reaction and understanding. Remember: For your client, this is about self-exploration, not self-explanation.

You may wonder, if you don't look at your client, how will you notice non-verbals? I find if I reduce eye contact in the beginning, a client soon stops looking for it, and then I can go back to observing without them being distracted. But this will vary considerably from client to client, and you may want to alter how much you engage in eye contact depending on how deep an inner-focused trance state you are looking to have them be in. If, for example, you are in a business coaching situation with a whole group of clients, you may not want to encourage a deeply inner-focused state.

Backtracking and Reviewing

Once you have identified several symbols in a landscape, help your client learn more about a particular symbol by zooming in for specific details or by zooming out to consider the broader context in which the object is located.

> *There is information in the specifics and in the whole.*

Remember the train model I described in the beginning? Imagine your client's attention is focused on the train that is on the track. You can zoom in to get details about the train, perhaps about what powers it. Or you can zoom out to consider the landscape the track is moving through and what else is nearby. By zooming in and out, you help your client attend to what they might not have noticed. There is information in the specifics and in the whole.

You can facilitate this zooming in and out so that your client follows you easily and experiences it smoothly by repeating a larger chunk of what your client has said. Notice below the subtle difference in purpose between backtracking and reviewing.

Backtracking   *To get back to a previous image or information*

- Your client may have given multiple details or images. You have developed one, and now you want to back to one you have not yet visited. Going back too abruptly, that is, making a huge leap back over a bunch of previously revealed information, can be disorienting for a client and snap them right out of the symbolic domain.

You may want to bring attention away from a negative to something more positive. (Example: To focus on the desired outcome or resource rather than a problem.)

Reviewing   *To keep the whole landscape alive and available to the client's mind/body*

- Recall the details about a symbol before you ask still more developing questions

- Slow a client down so they can sit with a feeling or situation longer

- Help the client keep a lot of information in mind

- Return the client to the symbolic domain, if something distracts or interrupts them

- Summarize the session as you are getting ready to end

Hints on Reviewing and Backtracking:

- **Reverse order**. To take your client back through their statements, as a general rule, go in reverse order; don't randomly mix up the details. Imagine the camera again: Jumping back and forth, up and down, among objects in a scene would be dizzying and break concentration.

- **Skip evenly**. You needn't repeat every detail nor every word. But if you are going to select some, skip in even intervals, such as repeating every third adjective, or select what seem like the key ones. Think of the camera again. You want to move evenly and fluidly.

- **Take your time**. Your client is likely visualizing the details you mention and experiencing the feelings that accompany them, so don't rush. You want this to be an embodied experience.

Reviewing and back tracking skills will become increasingly important as the length of your sessions increase and as we get to facilitating change. Work on developing a note-taking system that works for you so that you can accurately backtrack and review. In fact, we will be working on this next.

Example of Reviewing:

Reread the example on page 24 about the book. If I wanted to review some of the information so the client focuses on both the information and the feelings it evokes before answering the next question, I might say, with plenty of pauses:

Facilitator: And book... and you can leave it closed... or shut it.... and you open it when someone you want to be close to and trust. And when someone you trust, is there anything else about that trust?

TAKING NOTES

As you can now see, the amount of information you have to track and refer back to can be quite extensive! No doubt, with practice, you will develop your own system for taking notes. Some people write down very little, others quite a lot. You'll know you're recording too little when you can't accurately repeat back the exact words you want to repeat. You'll know you're recording too much when you aren't able to keep up with your client. Experiment with different amounts of information and different ways to organize it. You will gradually get a better feel for what information you will need again as you learn more about the strategies of where to direct attention.

As you learn: This note-taking strategy is not practical in a real session, but it is a great way to conceptualize backtracking and reviewing. It will to keep you from going too far afield from your chosen focal point. You can start this chart at any point; it doesn't have to be a desired outcome. Likewise, the developing questions in each circle are just *examples* you might choose; the point is what *content* you are asking about.

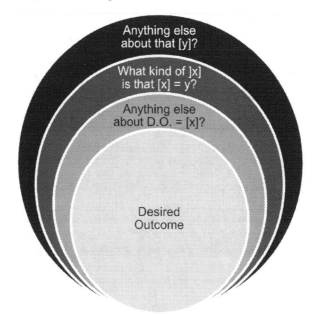

Derived from Caitlin Walker

• There is a larger, blank variation of this graphic on page 127. Make as many copies of it as you like, and use it for practicing.

• Decide what word/phrase you want to start with in the center. Any details that emerge with your questions about that word/phrase goes in the second circle; any details that emerge about something in the second circle go in the third, and so on with the fourth.

• When you get to the fourth circle, verbally **backtrack** your way to your starting word/phrase by repeating some of the details from **each** of the circles **in reverse order**. In so doing, you are reviewing the whole as well as getting back to the word/phrase fluidly.

• Now ask another developing question about something said in the first circle. Repeat the process.

For this next example, we will start filling in the center circle with the client's desired outcome.

Example:

Facilitator: And what would you like to have happen?

Client: *I'd like to be clearer about my college choice.* **(D. O.)**

Facilitator: And clearer about your college choice. And when clearer, that's clearer like what?

Client: *Like a clear ring around the right choice.* **(second circle out)**

Facilitator: And a clear ring around. And when a ring around, what kind of ring around' is that 'ring around'?

Client: *Like a ring around Saturn.* **(third circle out)**

Facilitator: And a ring around Saturn. And is there anything else about Saturn?

Client: *Yes, it makes me think of Greek mythology, for some reason. Mythology can seem like just a nice story with some magical elements, but it can have a deeper truth to it.* **(fourth circle out)**

You may decide it is time to head back to the center, before you get too far from this client's desired outcome for right now. Here is where you **backtrack,** going over the information in reverse order.

Facilitator: And a deeper truth....and Greek mythology....and Saturn...a ring around...a clear ring. And you want to be clearer about your choice. And when your choice, is there anything else about that choice?

Client: *Yes, I think my college choice has to come from a deeper place, a place that knows my truth.*

You can start this concentric circle sheet with anything: a desired outcome, a symbol, a word. It is a useful note-taking exercise because it will help you avoid a common problem for many beginners: they start off with one word and just keep going with a question about something that has just been said. Eventually, they are so far distant from where they started, they sense they've gotten lost. (Notice how the client made a connection between her college choice and the deeper truth when her attention was directed to review the whole? This doesn't always happen, but it can, for all the information is part of an inter-connected system.)

A few other suggestions about note-taking:

- Be sure you note the starting desired outcome statement in full. All its bits may be significant.

- If you are not using the circles, but some other form of note-taking, like outlining or webbing, be sure to write D.O., underline, or otherwise clearly identify desired outcomes when you hear them. This habit will help you notice them as they emerge, and will help you find them in your notes when you go back and mature the landscape (which we get to in *Basics Part Two*).

• If you want to keep track of your questions as well as the replies, you can use the first letter of each word in the question. Thus, "What would you like to have happen?" becomes WWYLTHH? (or HH?, for short) "Is there anything else about" becomes AE? "What kind of" is WKO? This is standard practice among Clean facilitators.

3.2 | *Activity*

Keep the list below in sight as you practice now with a client or partner. Take notes, using the chart on page 127. Write your client's desired outcome in the center, and use the concentric circles to develop information about words in your client's statement and their attributes. Or start your circle note-taking once you have a metaphor for the D.O.; put it in the center, and develop information about it. Or, better yet, do the exercise twice, and do both. Plan on spending about 10 minutes per round. Think you will run out of things to ask about? There's always more to ask about! Don't stop until your time is up.

Situating:
"Where would you like to be/me to be?"

Desired outcome:
"What would you like to have happen?"

Attributes of the desired outcome statement:
"What kind of [x] is that [x]?"
"Is there anything else about [x]?"

Take into metaphor:
"That's like what?"

Develop the metaphor:
"What kind of [x] is that [x]?"
"Is there anything else about [x]?"

After your practice as a facilitator, answer the following questions:

Something I did well was:

Something I want to work on next time is:

ENDING A SESSION

I trust you found ending your session just because time was up somewhat abrupt. Hopefully you are sensitized to the need to develop a better way to bring your client's session to a graceful stop. Consider the following suggestions for doing so *cleanly*.

How to End Gently

If your client has been deeply immersed in their metaphor landscape, it can be jarring to abruptly shift out of it. I think of it like deep-sea diving: you don't want to cause the bends by surfacing too quickly! You might choose one or more from among the following options for ending a session:

1. Change your voice to a more conversational tone and pace.

2. Refer to the person by name; this grounds a person and brings their attention back to the present moment.

3. After reviewing the highlights of the session, ask the Clean Language question you will be learning in the next chapter,

    "And what difference does knowing all this make?"

4. After you review the major information from the session, you could say, **"And as we have just a minute or two left in our session, is there anything else about all that for right now?"** (Know your client; there are some people who will take this as an open invitation to go on and on. This would not be an ending to use with such a client).

5. Ask, **"And would this be a good place to stop for today?"**

6. Invite: **"I invite you in the next days and weeks to take all the time you need to become more familiar with** [describe again a key resource]." Example: that confidence, there, in your spine like a mighty oak tree."

7. After a quiet pause in case something more is forthcoming, you can ask a question inviting a cognitive response. Example: **"So, how was that for you?"** or **"Anything you'd like to say about the session?"** You can be more conversational, but stay *clean*!

3.3 | *Activity*

Write out an ending or two you would like to use. It can be one of the above or one of your own, but remember, stay *clean*! Practice saying it aloud.

Post Session

Once the Symbolic Modeling session is finished, you may want to:

1. **Invite your client to share any thoughts or responses** to their experience, but stay clean. Don't offer comments, interpretations or advice about the metaphors. If you've conducted a full-blown Symbolic Modeling session, clients generally are re-entering reality from a slightly altered state. Most do not want to do much cognitive processing; they prefer to stay in their somewhat liminal state. Honor that more integrating is going on. The right time to develop an action plan or cognitively address what has come up might well be at another time/session. You should, however, talk enough to be sure that your client is grounded and focused enough to walk or drive safely.

2. **Invite them to draw a Metaphor Map:** This is a drawing of the metaphors from a session. Your client decides which details to include and which to leave out, if any. The picture:

   - Offers your client a way to remember the metaphor landscape.

   - Holds an emotional charge that keeps your client in touch with their inner experience.

   - There's no rule that says what your client draws has to be just what was said in the session. Metaphors continue to evolve even though you have finished the session. Let your client know it's okay to add any new details of which they becomes aware as they draw.

3. **Describe how to use their metaphors:** Your client's resource metaphors are not working only subconsciously after a session; clients can consciously draw upon the symbols in their daily lives. So, for example, if a client has discovered a mighty oak tree in their spine, remind them to call upon that image—to feel that tree again in their body, to visualize it (or however they experienced it in the session) when their confidence sags before making that presentation they came in worried about. Perhaps another client determined that relaxed was a calm ocean beneath their solar plexus. Encourage them to revisit that image the next time they have a problem relaxing.

   > *Don't offer comments, interpretations or advice about the metaphors.*

4. **Assign homework:** some of the many possibilities

   - Draw another metaphor map, as the one your client has now will evolve/change between now and your next session

   - If your client likes to journal, invite them to explore further in writing.

   - Try out a new behavior your client has identified as desirable.

No doubt, you will find your own way of integrating this with the work you already do. I do recommend honoring Clean Language's principles as they stand long enough to assess their validity, such as not offering any interpretations of metaphors. You may be surprised by how much can happen without your well-intended "interference"—and your client will feel empowered because they will feel it all comes from themselves.

When to End

Consider several possibilities:

1. You have run out of time.

2. Your client seems tired or expresses a desire to stop. They may open their eyes, establishing direct eye contact in a way that clearly marks a shift. They may adopt a more conversational one, or their content may become more cognitive-sounding rather than metaphoric. Your client may say something like, "Wow. I've got a lot to think about!" Or, "That was really interesting!" They make it clear that they are no longer in their symbolic domain.

3. Events in the metaphor landscape come to a logical resolution or resting place.

4. You have completed developing something particularly positive, such as a resource or a positive potential to consider. If you only have a short time remaining, it would not likely be helpful to your client to get started on something that appears to be complex and/or emotionally difficult.

FAQ | *Frequently Asked Questions*

What if I ask the wrong question or change my mind about what I want to ask?

Let it ride. Don't interrupt your client by saying "Oops!" or "What I meant to say was...". Just wait for your next opportunity to ask a question and backtrack to where you want to go. Sometimes, even with an awkward question, the client gets something helpful. If your client seems really stumped or confused, or looks at you directly as if they have "popped out" of their symbolic domain or metaphor world, you can just smoothly review and ask another question.

What if I miss an important opportunity?

Relax! At every moment, there are any number of directions you could direct attention, though some, granted, may be more helpful than others. You can't always tell where the gold lies! But, generally speaking, if it's important and you both missed it, it will come back again later with the same image or in a different guise. The subconscious is thrilled you're listening and will be heard!!

What if I am not comfortable with where my client wants me to sit?

Certainly, feel free to use your common sense. But as long as you are not endangered or cannot see or hear properly, do your best to adjust rather than ask your client to. And if your client wants to sit in your desk chair-- *yours!* -- can you be curious enough to see what might happen if they sit in the seat they associate with expertise or wisdom... or who knows what?

Section Three Summary

By focusing your client's attention on their desired outcomes, you flesh out and strengthen their vision of and commitment to how they would like things to be, rating that reinforce the problem state.

Giving your client the option to determine your situating arrangement begins the session, as they create the space in accordance with their inner knowing and needs.

Careful attention to facilitating technique subtleties such as eye contact, voice, emphasis, pacing, and non-verbals are key elements to leading your client in to a natural trance and their symbolic domain and for keeping them there.

Backtracking and reviewing information that has emerged is how you navigate around your client's metaphor landscape. They are also important for keeping the landscape active in your client's awareness.

Ending a session skillfully entails gently helping your client leave their symbolic domain and re-enter reality. It brings closure and leaves your client in a helpful place.

My take-away from this section is...

Questions I have...

3.4 | *Review Activity*

Recall the "open book" example. (See page 24). It's often a good idea to develop a bit of information about the desired outcome phrase *before* you take it into metaphor to help the client collect a fuller sense of what they want. With the following sentences, practice asking **at least two attribute questions** of a number of words in these desired outcome statements, and then ask **the metaphor question**.

CLQs: **"And what kind of** [selected detail x] **is that** [selected detail x]**?"**
"And is there anything else about that [x]**?"**
"And that's [x] **like what?"**

1. I want to lay out a detailed plan for my new business, so it has room to grow.

2. I need to have more insight into my strengths and weaknesses, so I can get the partner best suited to me.

3. I want to inspire people to join in my vision.

4. I wish I was more relaxed around other people.

5. I need to welcome change with open arms.

6. I want to be open to change.

PRACTICE OPPORTUNITIES

You can always go back to other chapters and re-purpose the sentences from previous exercises, such as looking for **desired outcomes** or practicing **attribute questions** or looking for **resource words to invite into metaphor.** As with learning to drive, to speak a new language or to play an instrument, the more you practice, the better you will become.

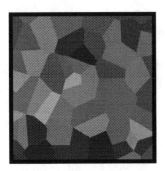

Section Four

*"We shall not cease from exploration
And the end of all our exploring
Will be to arrive where we started
And know the place for the first time."*

–T.S. Eliot

WHEN SPACE BECOMES PSYCHOACTIVE

We are going to step away from Clean Language now to briefly explore a variation on another technique developed by David Grove that he called **Clean Space**. Facilitators have discovered it can be used with many types of clients and in many contexts. You'll be delighted to hear that it's very simple to learn and facilitate.

> *Psychoactive space is filled with information from the client's inner experience.*

While we won't cover Clean Space in this book, I am offering you this exercise to give you a sense of how much information a *space* can "hold," so you can better appreciate the potential significance of the *location* of symbols.

Using Clean Language questions and directives, the space around a client becomes *psychoactive*, a term coined by David Grove to describe space filled with information from the client's inner experience with which they actively engage. As multiple spaces are explored, the client develops a *network of connections* between them, creating a *system*. As we've learned, when there is a change in one part of a system, all parts are affected. By physically moving from place to place, and repeatedly asking what is known from that space, the client explores the system as it learns from itself.

You may wonder what this experiential technique is doing in a book about mining your client's metaphors. Think of the physical space they move around in as metaphoric. As the client places a particular idea or feeling in one spot, and then another idea or feeling in another spot, they experience what the relationship between them is *like*. As they engage in this locating of information and exploring the spaces, much more about their system and all that's interconnected will emerge, often with surprising results.

You might use Clean Space to:

- consider the *whole* of a complex issue   (get a panoramic view)
- gain greater clarity on a *specific* detail   (get close up)
- see something from a *new perspective(s)*   (different camera angles)
- develop and compare options   (split screens)

By now you know that using what seems like a very simple technique on the surface can reveal information of great complexity. Many clients find the act of *moving* and *experiencing different viewpoints* very powerful. I've found this to be true particularly for people who describe themselves as primarily kinesthetic, perhaps because so many other techniques are primarily visual and/or language-based.

Note: If you want to learn more techniques using space and movement, see my book *Panning for Your Client's Gold: 12 Lean Clean Language Processes* (Find under Resources).

CLEAN SPACE FACILITATING TECHNIQUES

You'll be using the script on the next page to direct a session. Here are some tips for skillful facilitation.

- Clean Space is more directive than a Symbolic Modeling session. Use the imperative; in a neutral but firm manner, tell the client to "Find a space that…"

- When doing any exercise with your client using space, be aware of where you stand. Avoid walking across space between their named positions. It would be like walking across a field during a game; even if the players aren't in that part of the field, you would be in the "game space." Encourage the client at the start to indicate if you are too close for them to concentrate, too far away to feel your attention or to be heard, or in the way of finding a space(s).

- Do not write down anything for your client. Do not touch or move the Post-its yourself. Who knows what effect such kinesthetic involvement will have on the information your client discovers? (You may need to make adjustments to this rule if your client has a physical disability.)

- Avoid eye contact with your client. Look instead at the space you are directing attention to. As you extend your energy towards the space, it will help direct your client to do the same, and discourage conversation with you or explanations for your benefit. Remember: You want to encourage self-exploration, not self-explanation. The first-time client is liable to look at you, try to catch your eye, and do what they are used to doing when having a conversation with someone. But this, like a Clean Language session, is not about having a conversation. Encourage your client to attend to their inner self by not having a lot of eye contact with them, not saying yes or nodding, and so on.

This next activity is a variation on Clean Space. It's a shorter, more scripted exercise than the original, more open-ended Clean Space. In this variation, your client is invited to explore something they *want more of* in their life (presumably a *desired outcome*.)

When a client wants clarity on some issue, this is a great exercise you can do in 15-20 minutes. I also find that clients do not tend to go as deeply into an altered state in Clean Space processes, the way they are apt to when deeply engrossed in a Symbolic Modeling session. Thus, it is easier with this Clean Space exercise to do other, more cognitive work afterwards, like come up with an action plan. But I do say *tend*; naturally, every client is different, and you need to evaluate your client's needs as they unfold.

Follow the script precisely so you will stay *clean*.

Facilitator Script: "Enough" Psychoactive Space Activity

Facilitator: Select something you want more of in your life. (Identified as [x] in your script.) Now write on three Post-its the words "Enough," "Not Enough," and "More Than Enough." Put these Post-its where it feels right.

(These are generally placed on the floor, though sometimes clients will use furniture or the walls. Be sure to wait patiently until the client looks up at you, signaling they are satisfied with the placement and ready to move on. Ditto for every time they move to a new space.)

1. Stand on "Enough."
   And what do you know from there about Enough [x]?
   (Client answers all questions aloud. When they are finished and looks up at you, give the next direction.)

2. Now go to "Not Enough."
   And what do you know from there about Not Enough [x]?

3. Now go to "More than Enough."
   And what do you know from there about More than Enough [x]?"

4. Now go to between "Enough" and "Not Enough."
   And what do you know from there about [x]?

5. Now go to between "Enough" and "More than Enough."
   And what do you know from there about [x]?

6. Now find a space that knows about "Not Enough," "Enough," "More than Enough," and all that. (Make a sweeping gesture of all spaces.)
   "And what do you know from there about all this?"

7. And what difference does knowing all this make?

(Variation by James Lawley)

Further variation on this Clean Space activity: If you have the time, you might add one or two more Clean Language questions at any given spot. You could ask, "And is there anything else you know *from that space*?" Or pick out a key word [y] and ask, "And is there anything else about that [y]?" But ask only one or two questions at any one space! Grove's intention was that the client would not get bogged down in the information or the emotion in any one place. Much of the new learning comes from the *movement* and *relationship* between the spaces.

4.1 | Activity

Decide on something you want more of in your life. For example, it might be more relaxation, more adventure, more play, more time for yourself. Ideally, you will have a practice partner to read the facilitator's script. A session usually takes about 20 minutes. Give your answers aloud. *After the session,* use the space below to record what you discovered. Then take a turn as facilitator.

I would like to have more _____.

What I discovered in the space Enough:

What I discovered in the space Not Enough:

What I discovered in the space More than Enough:

What I discovered in the space between Enough and Not Enough:

What I discovered in the space between Enough and More than Enough:

What I discovered in the space that knows about All That:

What difference knowing all this makes:

Surprised by what you discovered? Yes, it's a remarkably simple, yet very powerful technique!

Clean Language Question #5: Identifying A Location

Now that you've experienced just how significant LOCATION and SPACE can be for the information they hold, we're going back to Symbolic Modeling. You should be primed for the next Clean Language question you will add to your tool box.

Once your client is in the symbolic domain (i.e. immersed in their world of metaphors) and after you have developed a few *attributes* to familiarize them with a metaphor that has emerged with "What kind of [x]?" and "And is there anything else about that [x]?" questions, you will want to *locate* the symbol in your client's psychoactive space with another developing question:

> **"And [x].
> And when [x],
> where/whereabouts is [x]?"**

You can use either *where* or *whereabouts*. Personally, I prefer *whereabouts*. To my ear, it flows more rhythmically and sounds less like ordinary speech than *where*. It also can suggest either "where in the vicinity" or "where more specifically." I like its open-ended quality. But either choice is considered correct. Experiment and see which you prefer. Get a facilitator to use both for you as a client, and find out if you *feel* a difference.

It's a good rule of thumb to ask this question at least **three times**, or until the client essentially repeats the information about the location, implying that's all they know, for now at least. Don't be fooled by an answer like, "It's in my heart," thinking then you have the answer. Keep going!

Example:

Client: *I feel a loving presence nearby.*

Facilitator: And a loving presence nearby. And whereabouts nearby is that loving presence?

Client: *It's in my heart* (closing their eyes.)

Facilitator: And it's in your heart. And when it's in your heart, whereabouts in your heart?

Client: *In the center.*

Facilitator: And in the center of your heart. And when center, whereabouts in the center?

Client: *Deep. It's very, very deep in the center. And there's a light there!*

There is often more information there than the client first realizes, if you just keep holding their attention on the location and zoom in for more detail.

When to Ask a Where/Whereabouts Question

If you are listening closely to your client's words and watching their gestures, you will often pick up on indications that a symbol has a location, or that a location is involved even before a symbol has revealed itself. In the example above, note the client uses the word *nearby*, suggesting they are already aware of a location, that the space around and/or inside them is *psychoactive*. It is within the *logic of the landscape*, then, to ask the location question. If they can't locate the metaphor, they may need more information. Go back to developing more attributes of the symbol.

Locating resources is particularly helpful and important to a client. Not only will locating the resource help them gather more information about it, but they will be able to find the resource again when they need it.

4.2	*Activity*

Practice asking the location question about words in the following sentences. Consider the logic of the landscape: What might reasonably have a place? What's the resource? Where/whereabouts is that resource? (Note: if a client has a feeling, they are feeling it somewhere. Locate it!)

Example:

Client: *I want my inner confidence to flow easily, like a mountain stream.*

Facilitator: And inner confidence flow easily, like a mountain stream. And when inner ...
                 and when flow like a mountain stream, whereabouts is that mountain stream?

CLQ   **"And where/whereabouts is that [x]?"**

1. I would like to access my innermost tenacity.

2. I'd like to feel very relaxed and confident about my presentation skills.

3. I want to trust implicitly that I can find my true purpose.

4. The artist in me is just waiting to burst forth!

5. There's a solid granite foundation under me.

6. I am a part of the Tree, the Tree of Life.

7. There's a path that leads to the Promised Land.

WORKING FROM A METAPHOR MAP

Having your client bring a metaphor map to start a session or ending a session with your client starting a new one are effective uses of a client's drawing, but you can also conduct a session using a map your client continues to draw on and develop as the session progresses—even on the phone.

One advantage of this technique for you both, at least in person, is that *the map holds the whole of the session in view at once.* You don't have to work as hard repeating what has been said before to keep it all actively in the session. Thus, you don't have as much need of note-taking either. The picture keeps track of things for you. And the map helps you both remain very aware of the location of symbols. Interestingly, it may reveal when something might be missing in its blank spaces.

I have often felt that the metaphors aren't quite as fluid at times when the client draws, as compared to a verbal session. Drawing seems to slow the process down, but this is not necessarily a bad thing! More is revealed and experienced, as the client takes time to draw and "sit with" the images, and sits with frustration, perhaps, if changes need to be made. They can always start a new drawing if one feels too static. Having scissors, tape and Post-its on hand can be helpful for clients, who can get quite creative making a drawing change in response to their landscapes' needs! If you have one available, using a white board works wonderfully, as changes are so easy to make.

Helpful Hints:

- Don't touch a client's drawing. Gesture gently towards it with the palm side of your hand. Most people find direct pointing harsh and feel it as an intrusion into their psychoactive space. When you are gesturing towards an area, move your hand out of the way as soon as where you're directing attention is clear, so your hand is out of your client's line of vision and less apt to be a distraction.

- Stay as clean as possible. Sometimes on the phone you may have to add a few words such as to the left or in the bottom right. Listen closely for the words your client is using, like *above* or *on top, below* or *at the bottom,* and try to stay as close to their language as possible.

- Don't let the drawing distract you! You can get caught up in the images, and forget to develop the basics, ask for attributes, desired outcomes, etc., just like you do in a verbal session.

- Some clients resist doing a drawing, feeling they have to be artistic and will be judged. You might want to use the words sketch or doodle instead. Call it play. Or, with a new client, let it go until you have developed more of a relationship with the client. After all, the purpose is not to get your client to make a drawing; it is to help your client access their inner experience and wisdom. You have other tools in your toolbox if your client is not comfortable drawing.

Times you might try using metaphor maps during the session:

1. When a client struggles to get into metaphor; a drawing is a first step into symbol.

2. When a client repeatedly drifts out of metaphor, keeps "going cognitive."

3. When a client flits from metaphor to metaphor to metaphor, rather than developing any one. (This is different than multiple metaphors emerging as the landscape expands.)

4. When a client drifts off, loses focus, gets sleepy, has trouble staying with the process.

5. When a client likes moving, describes themselves as kinesthetic or artistic.

6. When your client is a child. (But don't think for a minute adults don't find this helpful and fun!)

7. When you want to slow the client down.

8. When you want to hold the whole of the landscape before the client.

9. When you find it helpful to have the drawing holding the space and recording details, assuming your client is happy working this way, of course.

10. When your client likes to have a record of sorts of the session. A drawing of a resource can be a wonderful thing to put up at home and draw inspiration from!

Getting your client drawing

So, what's a clean way of inviting a client to start a drawing? First, be sure you have materials ready and a cleared surface to draw on. (I find most people prefer magic markers. Copy paper is fine, though I like having an unlined flip chart around as an option, in case my client wants a larger drawing space.) You can also use a white board, which makes changes wonderfully easy to make as the landscape evolves, and is easily recorded by both your phone cameras for your records. It does, however, limit color options.

No doubt you will find your own invitational phrase, but you could try:

A conversational start: "Would you like to use drawing to explore that?" ...and gesture towards the blank paper and markers.

Or

"And [x]. And when [x], that's [x] like what?" or "And that would look like what?", gesturing towards the paper and markers and looking expectant.

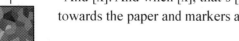

Here are a few more Clean Language questions that are useful for when you are facilitating a client who continuously adds to their drawing throughout the session. You will notice, like the basic CLQs you have been learning, they are simple and brief.

Throughout the session, when the client mentions a new symbol or a new attribute for one already drawn, you can ask,

> **"And whereabouts could that[x] be?"**

If they need a prompt to draw the new information, rather than just saying it aloud, the standard Clean directive is,

> **"And put that down."**

....or, once they get the hang of it, just gesture to the paper, looking expectant.

If a picture is well-developed, and there is a blank area—ask about it!

> **"And"** (gesture to a blank area).
> **"And what could be there?"**

In this way, you keep the drawing developing along with the emerging information.

If you are an art therapist or, for any other reason, are particularly interested in using drawing throughout a session, I suggest you attend an in-person training to master this skill, as there is more to it than I can convey here. There is a real art to keeping the information emerging on the paper while encouraging the client to simultaneously experience the metaphor landscape in or around their body. It makes for a powerful session. But, even without practice with the subtleties, the information above will give you a good start.

4.3 | *Activity*

Practice now with a partner. Look back to Section Two where you developed three resources of your own. Alternate facilitating each other to gather more information about each one. Be sure to include locating them! You can start conversationally with something like, "And would you like to describe what you know about your [resource]?" or with a more formal CLQ to set the tone and invite a mindful state:

> *"And what do you know now about that [resource]?"*

During each round, the client is adding whatever information emerges to their existing map or starts a new one. We call this **updating your metaphor map**.

What did you discover about each of your resources? You may want to answer in words, pictures, or both.

#1

#2

#3

Section Four Summary

Space becomes psychoactive when the client projects their inner experience into it and engages with it actively.

Clean Space is a technique that invites a client to explore their psychoactive spaces and the relationship between them.

Locating a symbol or resource helps a client learn more about it and helps them to access it again when they need it.

Metaphor maps are drawings of a client's symbols located in relationship to one another. They can be used at the beginning, at the end, or throughout a session. Metaphor maps are helpful reminders of what is in the landscape, keeping the symbols and accompanying emotions active in your client's system. Drawing can also help your client discover new information.

My take-away from this section is...

Questions I have...

4.4	*Activity*

Practice developing metaphors with CL attribute questions. Assuming your client has made the following statement, respond, using full syntax (three parts). Be sure the second part ("And when....") directs attention to where or what your question will be about. If you are practicing with a partner playing a client, have them answer the selected question, and you continue on, asking two or three more developing questions of their answers. I suspect the client will discover that, even when they begin with someone else's statement just read off the page, with just a few personal answers, they will discover something will emerge with personal significance or emotional resonance. It's kind of weird how that happens...

CLQs: **"And is there anything else about that [x]?"**

"And what kind of [x] is that [x]?"
"And where/whereabouts is that [x]?"

1. The shield would like to stay where it is, comfortable and easy.

2. My heart and Little Child are both inside that chrysalis.

3. It's like an engine that keeps me running.

4. There are a bunch of people near me on this big stage with lots of props.

5. There's a door in my tree house, and I want to get inside.

6. The knowing comes from multiple places that are all connected, like lights on a string.

7. It's been a long time since I felt like this, like I belong in this circle of people.

8. It's a radiating energy that sustains and protects me.

Section Five

*"Life can be pulled by goals
just as surely as it can be pushed by drives."*

–Viktor Frankl

THE P/R/O OF REPROCESS

"And what would you like to have happen?"

Remember this question? When you ask a client this, you are asking for what we call a *desired outcome*. This is the fundamental orientation the Symbolic Modeling process takes: guiding the client to become more familiar with their desired outcomes. But your client may or may not answer you directly. Your client will likely respond in one of four ways:

1. They will begin to tell you their story. Your client may feel they want you to know a bit about them, or they may want the relief of unloading all that they have been carrying. This is the type of information we refer to with the *E* of REPROcess: E for Explanations.

2. They will state a *problem*.

3. They will propose *a remedy to the problem*.

4. They will tell you how they would like it to be, their *desired outcome*.

The explanations you will largely set aside. The other responses each have a special way of being managed in a Symbolic Modeling session. Tompkins and Lawley developed this modeling strategy and have dubbed it P/R/O for short.

You will likely hear *P*roblems, *R*emedies, and desired *O*utcomes repeatedly throughout a session, both ones related to your client's everyday life and to their metaphors. Each type of answer suggests a different response.

Problem:
- *Something the client doesn't like*
- *It is usually stated in the present tense*
- *There is no desire/want expressed*

In response to a problem statement, first repeat the gist of the problem, acknowledging it as expressed and experienced by your client. It also gives them a chance to hear their own words again, to hold the whole of it in their mind and feel the accompanying feelings. Then ask the *desired outcome* question:

"And when [problem], what would you like to have happen?"

This moves your client's attention from what they *have* to what they *want*. Most people know a great deal about their problems, but often haven't given much consideration to what they would like instead. As a general orientation, in Symbolic Modeling, we direct attention away from problems and toward outcomes.

Example:

Client: *I don't like the way my doctor conducts my annual check-up.*

Facilitator: And you don't like the way your doctor conducts your check-up.
                           And when don't like the way your doctor conducts check-up, what would
                           you like to have happen?

Sometimes a client will respond with their desired outcome, will say what they want, but other times they may answer by describing what they don't want or what they want less of. In Symbolic Modeling, this is called a *remedy*.

Remedy:
* *A desire or need to have less of something*
* *It includes both a problem and a want*
* *It projects into the future*
* *It is a means to an end, not an end in and of itself*
* *It does not make clear what the results will be once the remedy has been accomplished*

When I was first learning the P/R/O model, Lawley and Tompkins' use of the word *remedy* confused me, because I hadn't really absorbed the concept of the distinction between finding a solution for a problem versus achieving a new outcome. If you suffer from the same challenge, and if it's any help, you might think of the **R** as being for *removing* or *reducing* the problem. It doesn't fit every Remedy, but most often it does.

The correct response to a remedy statement is a bit tricky, because you have to change the client's words slightly by *removing* the problem, and *restating* what they have said as if the problem has been solved, and then ask a new Clean Language question.

"And when [reworded remedy]**, then what happens?"**

An example will make this clearer. Let's start with this client again.

Example:

Client: *I don't like the way my doctor conducts my annual check-up.*

Facilitator: And you don't like the way your doctor conducts your check-up.
                           And when don't like the way your doctor conducts check-up, what would
                           you like to have happen?

Client: *I want my time with him to not be interrupted by phone calls or nurses checking in with questions.*

Notice the client has still not said what they want, only what they don't want. The aim is to help the client become aware of something desirable to have, not just something undesirable to have less of.

Example continued:

Facilitator: And not be interrupted. And when not interrupted, then what happens?

  (Note the remedy question phrasing removes the problem: client is no longer interrupted.)

Client: *Then I'll know he cares enough to really listen to me.*

Now both the facilitator and the client are clearer on the client's two desired outcomes. Yes, two! (1) to know their doctor cares and (2) to be listened to.

Helpful hint:

Spotting Remedies tends to be challenging at first. You tend to hear the 'want' or 'need' word and fail to notice that what follows is still about the problem.

My suggestion is to keep an ear out for words like "get rid of"... "less of"... "stop or quit"... "not be/not have". Can you think of other such words?

Desired Outcome:
- A want, desire, or need for more of something beneficial
- It projects into the future
- There's no reference to the problem

Once you have a desired outcome, you have completed the P/R/O cycle (at least until a new problem or remedy emerges.) The next step is to develop more information about specific words in the desired outcome statement by asking the attribute questions you have learned.

Example continued:

Client: *Then I'll know he cares enough to really listen to me.*

Facilitator: And know he cares enough to really listen to you. And when really listen, what kind of listen is that listen?

In Symbolic Modeling, you want to develop clarity and familiarity with the desired outcomes, not with the problems! It's your job as the facilitator to keep track of the desired outcomes and to keep your client focused on them. This isn't to say you ignore problems entirely, but as a beginner, focus on the desired outcomes. If you recognize in yourself a tendency to focus on your client's problems, notice going forward what a difference using P/R/O makes!

P/R/O BENEFITS

Getting in touch with their own knowing

The P/R/O strategy for working with your clients' information will help them get in touch with their own knowing and their own desires for what's right for them. For many people, that, in and of itself, is a great gift. Untangling problems, remedies, and outcomes can also bring greater clarity to a client's situation.

Exploring consequences

P/R/O modeling helps your client avoid investing time and energy into working on remedies whose consequences have not been thought through. Also, focusing on having or doing less of something can be discouraging if it means your client must give up something appealing. (Ever gone on a diet and found yourself thinking a lot about the food you can't have? How helpful is that?) By attending to the benefits they can enjoy, on the other hand, your client can create an inspiring vision that can motivate them.

Avoiding assumptions

P/R/O modeling prevents you from setting an outcome for your client based on your own assumptions and experience. If early on in your information gathering, you find yourself ready to interrupt your client's exploration, thinking to yourself, "I've seen this before"... "The best way to handle a case like this is"... "Lots of my clients have had success by"... "I know exactly what this client needs to do"... "The client needs to realize right now that"..., then you are likely guilty of :

1. Making assumptions about your client that may be inaccurate, for each individual is unique.

2. Assuming you know better than your client's inner wisdom what needs to happen next and how soon.

Give your client's mind/body system the opportunity to learn from itself.

3. Depriving your client's mind/body system of the opportunity to learn from itself. If a better course or cognition or behavior is obvious to you, it is probably also obvious to at least *a part* of the client. You may only be hearing from some other part when the client says, "I want to quit my job tomorrow!" or "I'm never going to speak to my mother again!"

Resist being the sage or the expert, and trust the process. I promise you, your clients will surprise you: you will realize you made some assumptions, and that they are smarter than you might think about what they need (even children). And they will be less resistant, more open to what they need to do, and feel more empowered if you allow the realizations to come from them. Unless, of course, *you* have a strong need to be the expert and encourage your clients to be dependent on you, in which case most likely, Symbolic Modeling is not appealing to you.

If you work with mentally ill clients, your clients' thinking may be distorted, but I believe you'll also be surprised about how wise they are about what they truly need, once they are not performing, trying to please, or shock you. I do caution, however, that you need to master these skills before doing a full-on Symbolic Modeling-only session with a mentally ill client given to irrational thinking.

Looping

Note that a client may not progress from problem to remedy to desired outcome in a predictable linear fashion. They may offer a desired outcome and a problem all in one sentence. They may go from a remedy back to the problem, or add another problem altogether! We call this looping. The client's system is learning from itself as it discovers new information, new problems, new perspectives, and new possibilities. Work through each problem and remedy as it arises until your client gets to a desired outcome(s).

Always be listening for P/R/Os, not just at the beginning when a client is describing their life situation, but throughout the session and in the metaphor landscape as well. Use the same questions in response.

Examples:

"I'm stuck at the bottom of a dark well."   (Problem)
"I want to get out of the well, but I can't."   (Remedy and repeated Problem)
"I want to be up in the sunshine."   (Desired Outcome)

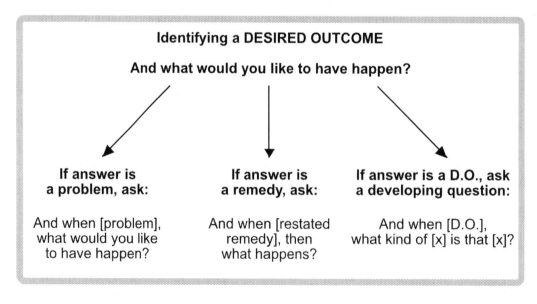

Identifying a DESIRED OUTCOME

And what would you like to have happen?

If answer is a problem, ask:	**If answer is a remedy, ask:**	**If answer is a D.O., ask a developing question:**
And when [problem], what would you like to have happen?	And when [restated remedy], then what happens?	And when [D.O.], what kind of [x] is that [x]?

Develop an aptitude for discriminating between problems, remedies, and desired outcomes, so you can keep directing your clients' attention to their outcomes. If you are wondering if you can ever 'legitimately' address problems with Clean Language, the answer is yes. We will get to that in *Basics Part Two: Facilitating Change,* when you learn CLQs and strategies for when clarity alone doesn't bring about the change a client wants.

5.1 Activity

Identify each of the following statements as likely representing a **Problem**, **Remedy**, or **Desired Outcome**. Remember: A Remedy states want your client wants to be rid of as well as what they desire, and a Desired Outcome states the result they want. Write out the question you would ask, using full syntax. You can use the chart on the previous page to help you remember the questions.

1. I'm sick of my 9–5 job!

2. I want to start exercising regularly again.

3. I want to write three really satisfying pages a day in the novel I'm working on.

4. I want to get out of this poisonous relationship.

5. I want to get over my writer's block.

6. I want to quit working at mindless, boring, repetitive tasks.

7. I feel suffocated in my marriage.

8. I want to lose 20 pounds.

9. My creative juices seem to have dried up!

10. I'd like to find the courage to tell my spouse I want a divorce.

11. I want a career where I feel I can make a difference in the world.

12. I hate to admit it, but I'm overweight.

Answers: (1) Problem (2) Desired Outcome (3) Desired Outcome (4) Remedy (5) Remedy (6) Remedy (7) Problem (8) Remedy (9) Problem (10) Desired Outcome (11) Desired Outcome (12) Problem

5.2 | *Activity*

Notice anything about the relationship between the examples in Activity 5.1? There are three sets of problem/remedy/outcome statements, a logical progression of answers a client might give. See if you can group them into their logical sets (answers below), then write two sets of statements of your own.

Set #1:

Set #2:

Set #3:

My #1:   Problem Statement:

               Remedy Statement:

               Desired Outcome Statement:

My #2:   Problem Statement:

               Remedy Statement:

               Desired Outcome Statement:

Answers for P/R/O sets: 1,6, 11; 7, 4, 10; 9, 5, 3; 12, 8, 2

METAPHORS CAN HAVE DESIRED OUTCOMES

Clients aren't the only ones in a landscape that can have Desired Outcomes. Some metaphors have Desired Outcomes, too. Concentrate on identifying symbols in the landscape that are personified, that is, that behave like living beings in that they have awareness, intentions and/or desires of their own. You can ask the same questions of them that you do of the client.

Interesting things happen when a metaphor's desired outcome either agrees with or conflicts with the clients or other symbols' desired outcomes. You will learn more about this is the *Basics Part Two* workbook.

Example:

Client: *I see myself floating in a canoe on a quiet lake. But I hear the voice of the waterfall roaring, and I'm beginning to feel the current pull me towards it!*

Facilitator: And a quiet lake, and a canoe, and waterfall, and current. And when a canoe, and the waterfall, and the current pulls, what would Waterfall like to have happen?

Client: *Oh, Waterfall doesn't want me to get hurt! It's just doing its thing. It wants to warn Current not to pull the canoe towards it!*

Facilitator: And Waterfall doesn't want you to get hurt! And wants to warn Current. And when Current, what would Current like to have happen?

Helpful Hint:

When I'm taking notes, I often start capitalizing a symbol that has become personified so as to remind myself to be aware of its desired outcomes and role as a perceiver and actor in the narrative. I listen for and/or ask about its own wants and intentions. In this case, I capitalize Waterfall and Current, since Waterfall has a voice and is getting ready to communicate with Current, suggesting the client's system knows Current, too, is personified.

5.3 | *Activity*

Practice writing and saying aloud the desired outcome question of symbols in these sentences taken from other practices. Just goes to show you, there isn't one right next question!

CLQ: **"And** [phrase including symbol]. **And when** [symbol], **what would** [symbol] **like to have happen?"**

Example:

Client: *There's a lake over there and a dam over there, and water is struggling. He's not where he feels he belongs!*

Facilitator: And there's a lake there and a dam there, and Water is struggling and not where he feels he belongs! And when Water is struggling, what would Water like to have happen?

1.   I see a black orchid. She seems pretty, but she's not.

2. There's an otter in the river who says he can help me.

3. I know I can cross this bridge, even though I'm scared. The bridge seems confident I can, too.

4. There's a sad little boy and a big white dog who's worried about him.

EXPLANATIONS

Now is a good time to recall our acronym REPROCess, and consider the *E* for explanations. Clients often start giving a lot of information when they tell you about problems; after all, it's probably what they've given the most thought to. They may want to fill you in on their past histories, particularly if this is their first session, and they don't yet know how different your approach is compared with many others. I find clients who have done a lot of personal development work or have had therapy before tend to want to analyze or otherwise explain their feelings, actions, etc., or they simply expect you need to hear it all.

The histories may be helpful (though probably not as much as you or your client may think), and certainly you want to be screening for clients with whom you are not qualified to work or who need another kind of support, such as medication. The analyses clients provide are not so helpful, for you or for them. These are a waste of your precious, limited time, because sometimes they hit the mark, sometimes they are off-base, and always they are occurring in the cognitive realm, not in the subconscious mind/body where the deeper wisdom lies. All that is relevant will be revealed in metaphor, both more precisely and more comprehensively than with cognitive analyses, which are rife with assumptions. Often these very assumptions are part of the problem.

Metaphors reveal which issues are connected with which other issues (and the results are often quite surprising!) When you focus your client's attention on metaphor, you avoid the irrelevant.

> *When you focus your client's attention on metaphor, you avoid the irrelevant.*

You want to be wary of getting sucked into these explanations, because the past is not the problem; the whys are not the problem. People are stuck in patterns they don't want because of how their mind/bodies process. I think you will be surprised to find, as you work with clients and Symbolic Modeling, just how little the content really matters. It is about the *hows*.

How does the client do decision-making? *How* does the client do depressed? *How* does the client know what they want? *How* does the client relax when stressed? *How* does the client maintain awareness of the resources they need to tap into? Working at the level of process, not content, means solutions are more apt to generalize, to encompass multiple parts of the client's history and/or issues. When you work at the process level, you work more comprehensively.

> *The past is not the problem. The whys are not the problem. It's about the hows.*

There's a skill to being able to gently redirect a client who is spending too much time in explanations, and it's not something I can give you an easy one-size-fits-all-situations solution for. You may need to make a judgment call; sometimes clients come at a moment of crisis, and they need to unload a bit. It's a question of when it's too much, and you have to use your own experience to determine that. Listen carefully for *desired outcome statements* and *resourceful embedded metaphors* to ask about, for they are often present in the explanations, and you can easily miss them unless you are on the look-out. Steer the client's attention to them with your questions. Get them into their body and out of the past... or out of the book or movie or song or poem— anything they're telling you about that's *someone else's* story or metaphor. No matter how much it resonates with them, how will you separate out what is relevant only to the other person and what is relevant for the client? Can the client even sort them out?

5.4 | Activity

Practice facilitating a 20 minute session with a client or practice partner. Your attention for this activity should be on listening for P/R/O: problem/remedy/outcome. Give yourself permission to take all the time you need to process an answer, decide if it falls into one of the categories, and recall which question to ask. You can use the chart on the next page to help you.

Something I did well was:

Something I want to work on next time is:

DEVELOPING A DESIRED OUTCOME LANDSCAPE

1. Establish a Desired Outcome

   Response to a Problem   **And what would you like to have happen?**

   Response to a Remedy   **And when [reworded remedy], then what happens?**

2. Develop the Desired Outcome

   Attributes   **What kind of [x] is that [x]?**

       And is there anything else about that [x]?

3. Elicit a metaphor for the Desired Outcome

   Metaphor   **And that's like... what?**

4. Develop attributes of the metaphor

   Attributes   **And what kind of [x] is that [x]?**

       And is there anything else about that [x]?

   Location   **And whereabouts is that [x]?**

Be listening for any additional problems, remedies, and desired outcomes that arise while developing information.

You may need to loop through the process again.

Section Five Summary

Clients don't always present a desired outcome when asked for one. With real life issues and in metaphor, they may present problems or remedies. The facilitator's job is to redirect the client towards desired outcomes.

Both clients and metaphors/symbols in the landscape can have desired outcomes.

Clients' explanations of their stories and their analyses of their issues are rarely as helpful as you might expect. Clean Language looks not to the past and the whys, but to the hows of clients' patterns.

My take-away from this section is...

Questions I have...

5.5	*Review Activity*

Identify each statement as a problem, a remedy, or a desired outcome, and write the correct question in the space.

Problem: "And when [x], **what would you like to have happen?**"

Remedy: "And when [reworded x], **then what happens?**"

Desired Outcome: "And when [x], **what kind of [x] is that [x]?**" **(or any other developing question)**

1. I want my wife to quit nagging me.

2. I want to feel I am contributing in a meaningful way.

3. I want to get the fountain in my gut running again.

4. I'm constantly butting heads with my teenager.

5. I'm determined to reduce my expenses each week until I get out of debt.

6. I want to stop doing work that doesn't fulfill me.

7. I want to make communicating with my son more pleasant.

Answers: (1) Remedy (2) Desired Outcome (3) Desired Outcome (4) Problem (5) 2 Remedies (6) Remedy (7) Desired Outcome

Section Six

"Who looks outside, dreams;
who looks inside, awakes."

–Carl Jung

THE FINAL DEVELOPING QUESTIONS

You're in the home stretch. We have three more basic Clean Language questions left to add to your list. While the questions you have learned so far could conceivably be all you need to facilitate clarity, the ones covered here lend a depth and richness to the landscape that emerges. They often elicit crucial information that may lie dormant without them.

Clean Language Questions #6 and #7: Time and Sequence

Recall that problems are happening in the present, and remedies and outcomes are future-oriented. This is a fine segue to introducing the importance of the next Clean Language questions you will add to your list of basic questions, those concerning time.

You have used one of them already with remedies to explore consequences, which is just one reason to develop a time sequence. Another reason is to find out what happens *before or after* an event, feeling, or thought, so that you can help your client learn more about their mind/body system or response/behavior patterns.

To use a spatial metaphor, you have been developing your client's landscape *vertically*, asking more information about given details. You can also develop it *horizontally*, over time, by asking:

Before: **"And when [x], what happens just before [x]?"**
After: **"And when [x], then what happens?"**
            or
            "And when [x], what happens next?"

Ask time questions to help a client:

*   Develop more context for [x]
*   When there is a missing piece in the logic of the landscape
*   Get a different perspective
*   Notice choice points for doing something different
*   Explore consequences

Time questions can help:

*   Make manageable that which seems overwhelming by breaking it down into smaller chunks
*   Slow down the client who is rushing to action without gathering information first (the before question)
*   Explore consequences of an action (the after question)
*   Develop a plan of action

Metaphors and Time Questions

Look for sequences to emerge in metaphor landscapes, too. These may be internal sequences of thoughts and feelings, external sequences of events and/or actions, or both.

Example:

Client: *I know I can withstand this storm, even though the winds around me are strong.*

Facilitator: And you know you can withstand this storm. And when withstand, that's withstand like what?

Client: *Like I'm a tree, a palm tree.*

Let us imagine you have helped the client develop more information about the palm tree, and now you want to develop still more context for this resource so the client can experience it and know what they gain by having this resource. This will help their system learn when it might be useful to call upon in the future.

Facilitator: And a tall palm tree, 20 feet high, in your spine, right in back. And you know you can withstand this storm. And when know you can withstand this storm, what happens *just before* that know?

Client: *I concentrate on the bottom of my spine. It's where the roots are. Deep roots.*

Facilitator: And deep roots, the bottom of your spine. And when deep roots and a tall palm tree right in back, then what happens?

Client: *Then I know the wind can blow, and the palm tree can bend, but I'll still be okay, because the roots will hold me fast. When the storm passes, the tree will stand upright again.*

I love it when this happens! I doubt the client noticed the embedded metaphor in her first statement: that she could *withstand* the storm....and at the end, her tree is *standing* upright. There's wisdom in the precise words the client chooses, which is why we repeat them *exactly*. The metaphor lies just beneath the surface, a few Clean Language questions away!

6.1 | *Activity*

Practice developing information about these client statements with time questions. Expand on what you know about what happens *before* and *after* any given moment.

CLQs: "And [x]. And when[x], what happens just before [x]?"
         "And when [x], what happens next?"
         or
         "And when [x], then what happens?"

1. There's a lake over there and a dam over there, and the water is almost to the top.

2. I feel excited and curious, but I'm a little worried too.

3. There are people on the shore yelling to me to come out.

4. Now my mother is hugging me. There are tears in her eyes, and she's laughing.

5. Whenever I try to move forward, I hold myself back.

6. Sometimes I think I can meet my goals; sometimes I feel I can't.

Clean Language Question #8: Source

The next basic developing question asks the client to consider the source of a symbol or feeling. You do this by asking,

"And where/whereabouts could that [x] come... from?"

With all the symbols in a landscape to pick from, which would be good to use this question with? Let the logic of the landscape suggest opportunities. A great place to start is with resources.

Example #1:

Client: *It's such a good feeling, this love.*

Facilitator: And such a good feeling, this love. And when this love, where could this love **come from?**

Client: *From my heart, my open heart.*

Example #2:

Client: *I have some scissors in my knapsack, there behind me.*

Facilitator: And a knapsack, behind you. And scissors. And when scissors, where could those scissors **come from?**

Client: *An old woman brought them to me. She knows me well; she knows what I need.*

Practical Applications to Real Life Situations

What about practical applications? Again, resources are good to ask source questions about.

Example:

Client: *I need to energize my business with some new ideas if I'm to stay competitive.*

Facilitator: And need to energize your business and new ideas. And when new ideas, where could those new ideas **come from?**

Client: *From our project teams; they're who I depend on to come up with ideas.*

Facilitator: And project teams. And is there anywhere else those new ideas could **come from?**

Client: *Well, I guess we could study our competitors more. That might spark some thoughts.*

Facilitator: And project teams, And competitors. And is there anywhere else those new idea could **come from?**

Client: *I hadn't thought about it until you just kept asking, but we could ask our clients! Maybe run some focus groups.*

Keep going until your client runs out of ideas, then circle back and further develop each idea with questions like:

> And what kind of competitive is that competitive?
> And when new ideas, what kind of new is that new?
> And when focus groups and clients, what kind of clients are those clients?

Or guide the session into metaphor, and ask...

> And that's energize your business like what?
>
> And when spark some thoughts, that's spark like what?

You are conducting a brainstorming session with just your client's wisdom to tap. The Clean Language questions will often help them discover many more ideas than they ever realized they had!

6.2 | *Activity*

Practice writing out and asking aloud the source question of words in the following sentences. (If you're thinking, "But I would want to ask other CLQs first!", don't worry about it. This is just for practice.)

CLQs: "And where could that [x] come... from?"

1.   There is a radiant light that is warm and loving.

2.   We need some real outside-of-the-box thinking to develop some new software.

3. I feel really hopeful about my latest inspiration.

4. If I had a tractor, I could plow the Field of My Dreams.

5. With greater confidence, I could speak to a large audience with ease.

6. I need a different set of operating principles in my mental control center.

7. I want to allow myself to speak my truth, to say what it is I truly need.

8. There's an otter in the river who says he can help me, and there's a strong current, too.

Clean Language Question #9: Determining Relationships

I have saved this basic developing question for last because:

1. You need to have a reasonably well-developed landscape before it makes sense to ask it, and the other questions help you do that.

2. You don't use the relationship question often, though when you do, a major shift can occur. This is because it is in the relationship between metaphors that much of their significance lies.

Symbols standing alone are simply that—symbols. It is in their dynamic relationship with other symbols—their context, interactions, and the narrative they create—that meaning is made. Often these relationships emerge as your client describes what they notice and as they consider their desired outcomes.

But as more information emerges in the metaphor landscape and it increases in complexity, your client may not always notice the relationships among symbols. It is your job to be considering those relationships, and how they might be serving or hindering your client. You can draw your client's attention to them by asking:

> **"And [x]. And [y].**
>
> **And when [x] and when [y],...**
>
> **is there a relationship between that [x] and that [y]?"**

Use this question when you get a keen sense from the *logic* of the metaphor landscape that there is likely to be a relationship. If you start peppering your facilitation with a lot of relationship questions, two things can happen. First, if the client has to struggle to find a relationship, they will "go cognitive," that is, they will search outside the symbolic domain for a rational connection. Second, if they frequently *don't* find a relationship, your client is going to start feeling like you don't "get them" (i.e. you will weaken rapport). And you will have created a distraction.

Avoid implied assumptions

You are asking *if there is* a relationship, not what it is. Be sure to keep your tone curious so as not to imply that there should be a relationship. You are just checking in.

Example:

Client: *I want to care for myself, nurture myself more.*

(Imagine we fast forward 15 minutes, and the client describes going to a spa. I sense that she has not noticed that she has, indeed, made this effort to care for herself, and I am thinking that she might benefit from acknowledging herself for doing so.)

Client: *I went to a spa on Thursday. I've never done that before. I treated myself to a massage. It felt so good. Someone else was touching me in such a soothing, helpful way. It felt good to be cared for!*

Facilitator: And a spa and a massage. And it felt so good to be cared for. And when cared for .... and when you want to care for yourself, nurture yourself more, is there a relationship between treat yourself to a massage and that nurture yourself more?

Client: *Yes. I hadn't thought of it that way before, but yes. And I'm nurturing myself without adding calories!*

I used my client's *exact* words from earlier in the session. (Did you notice how she used the same phrase *care for* in both sentences? Beyond the logic of the content, that was a clue that these might be closely related. You may wonder if it's too big a leap—15 minutes. Will the client remember? If your question adheres closely to your client's words and logic, they are likely to make that leap with you with no problem. Be sure to pace your question *slowly*, especially when you're asking the client to go back to previously mentioned information. Give them time to make the leap mentally before you ask the relationship question.

Now you can see why it is so important to keep notes (or have a great memory.) You may want to use exact words again later—particularly those that relate to desired outcomes and resources.

Develop attributes first

Ask the relationship question *only after* your client has information about *both* symbols. Without attribute and location information developed, the client may "go cognitive" to analyze a possible relationship or they are likely to say, "I don't know." You should sense a relationship exists from the logic of the client's landscape before asking the question; you want to *follow* the client, not *lead* them.

When to use a relationship question

For starters, you might be looking for situations where being aware of a *relationship* might aid in achieving a desired outcome, either by drawing attention to how a resource might be useful or by revealing a problem that needs addressing.

Example of a logical connection:

Facilitator: And a fountain and a dam and a canal. And canal is dry, and you'd like it to be filled with water. And when a fountain and a dry canal, is there a relationship between that fountain and that dry canal?

The logic of the landscape may imply a relationship; it's the logic of what an object does or how it works that suggests the relationship (i.e. engines need fuel, transportation can move you from one place to another, shade provides protection from the sun, plants need water to survive, fountains have water, etc.)

> *Stick closely to the logic of the client's landscape.*

Sometimes a client implies a relationship just by juxtaposing two things with one another in time or space. Or the client may use a word(s) that suggest a relationship like *connect* or *deciding is both inside and outside*.

You might also ask the relationship question when:

- You are puzzled: how does this work/fit/make sense?

- One of the symbols might be a resource for the other

Example of a potential useful resource:

Facilitator: And you are tied to the tree…and a rope…and scissors in your knapsack, *and* you want to get loose. And when tied, and a rope and scissors, is there a relationship between that rope and those scissors, when you want to get loose?

But do this sparingly! You don't want to intrude on your client's landscape with all kinds of implied suggestions about how *you* would manage things. You want to keep to an absolute minimum the number of times a client will find themselves saying, "No, there's no relationship to [y]." It breaks your empathetic connection and the client's concentration.

Landscapes have a way of having their own dream-like logic, and what seems obvious to you, the client may already know will not work. Then again, your question may reveal a new problem that needs addressing. So don't worry if your relationship question seems to be pointing out the obvious. It may not be so obvious to the client, who has so much going on.

Example where a new problem emerges:

Client: *Knowing is in two places, in my head and in my gut.*

Facilitator: And knowing…in your head…and in your gut. And is there a relationship between that knowing in your head…and that knowing in your gut?

Client: *Actually, they're not connected, and that's not working for me.*

6.3 | *Activity*

Practice asking relationship questions of words in these sentences. This is bound to be somewhat artificial because you don't have the context of a well-developed landscape. Naturally, in a real session, you would be likely to ask some developing questions first, but this is for practice, so just go with it.

Include plenty of repetition of the words first to help the client consider *both* things you are directing attention towards. (I have made these statements wordier to help prepare you for real clients, who sound more like this. Remember, you don't have to repeat every word! Using full syntax, you can start to reduce the words you say as you focus in on the key ones your question asks about.) Practice phrasing the questions and asking them with a slow, inviting rhythm.

CLQs: **"And** [x]. **And** [y].
          "And when [x]...**and when** [y], **is there a relationship between that** [x] **and that** [y]?

1. I'm trying to control this boat that has two white sails with red stars, and the wind is blowing hard.

2. I'm standing in an orchard, and there's an ache in my chest, in my heart chakra. There's a void, and I want to fill it with abundance—like a cornucopia.

3. I'm trapped in a well, deep down, and I want to get out! At the top I can hear someone singing, like he's just doing his work, humming along.

4. I've been working a lot of overtime recently. And then my spouse has been so demanding that I'm completely stressed out!

5. I realize I need to be kinder to myself; I am such a perfectionist! Sometimes when I pray, I feel God's love, and I feel at peace.

6.4 Activity

Practice facilitating a 20 minute session with a client or practice partner. Your attention this time should be focused on asking **time**, **source**, and **relationship** questions, but you'll need all your questions. You may have to force the relationship question a bit; really logical opportunities just don't come up all that often, especially in short sessions. So, just practice asking one for the sake of trying, and don't worry so much about logic. Let your client know to expect that.

CLQs: **"And what happens just before [x]?"**
"And then what happens?"
"And what happens next?"

"And where could [x] come from?"

"And when [x] and when [y], is there a relationship between [x] and [y]?"

Afterwards, answer the following questions:

Something I did well was:

Something I want to work on next time is:

FAQ Frequently Asked Questions

Can clients do sessions for themselves?

You may be wondering and clients may ask, will they learn skills over the course of repeated sessions that they can apply for themselves? Once clients learn to access their own metaphors, they can usually do so easily. They can apply the same questioning process to themselves as you do in your sessions. They are likely going to get better and better at using the questions to get clarity—to learn more details and to consider aspects of their information they might never have pursued before. I've had clients who particularly like applying Clean Language questions to their dreams.

But for a full-on Symbolic Modeling session, most people find it far easier and more effective to have a facilitator asking the questions and steering the session. When you do it for yourself, you are having to manage both the mind/body, visceral experience of exploring your subconscious inner world *and* consciously and cognitively managing all the information that emerges—noticing P/R/O, strategizing how all the pieces of the landscape might be fitting together and where it needs and wants to go. That's a lot to try to do at once!

As your client's facilitator, you hold the space, keep track of all the information that emerges, and select questions so your client can concentrate on being in the experience itself. And when your client's primary goal is to change the status quo (which we'll cover in *Basics Part Two*), it may be just what your client does not notice themselves that keeps them stuck.

That said, if you have clients who want to facilitate themselves, you might encourage them to get my book, *Hope in a Corner of My Heart,* which recounts in detail 12 sessions I had with a client and includes a Clean Language activity at the end of each chapter for readers interested in self-exploration. You may find it to be a great practice tool, as well. (Find under Resources.)

Section Six Summary

Time questions are used to develop a sequence of thoughts, feelings, and/or actions and events. They are particularly helpful in identifying important moments of shift or choice points.

Source questions can be used to explore both internal and external resources.

Exploring **relationships** between symbols may aid in achieving desired outcomes by drawing attention to how a resource might be useful or by revealing a problem that needs addressing.

My take-away from this section is...

Questions I have...

6.5 | Review Activity

Start by identifying an *embedded* metaphor word associated with a desired outcome in each example. Working with a partner (or playing both roles yourself), invite your client/self to take that word into metaphor by asking:

"And [x]. And when [x], that's [x] like...what?"

Then develop information about the metaphor with the nine basic CLQs, using the chart on the opposite page for help. (Note: If you count 11 questions in the chart, it's because the "Then what happens?" appears twice, and a variation is included for the 'time forward' question.) With so many questions to use, you will likely need plenty of room to take notes, so I leave you to use your own paper.

1. I want to find the courage to leave my current job and find a new one.

2. I'm determined to adopt a healthy-eating life style.

3. I want to feel more energized about my new work project.

4. I yearn to discover my soul's true calling.

5. I want to track down the underlying cause of my headaches.

6. I want to embrace change as a positive thing in my life.

7. I'm sick of feeling like I'm dragging myself around all the time. I want to feel up-beat— at least most of the time.

Afterwards, answer the following questions:

Something I did well was:

Something I want to work on next time is:

CLEAN LANGUAGE

The basic CLQs where [x] stands for a client's words or non-verbals.

P/R/O
And what would you like to have happen?
And then what happens?

METAPHOR
And that's [x] like what?

ATTRIBUTES
And is there anything else about that [x]?
And what kind of [x] is that [x]?

LOCATION
And where/whereabouts is [x]?

TIME BEFORE
And what happens just before [x]?

AFTER
And then what happens?
And what happens next?

SOURCE
And where could [x] come from?

RELATIONSHIP
And when [x] and when [y], is there a relationship between [x] and [y]?

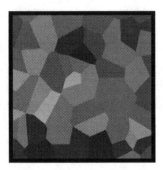

Section Seven

"The discovery of the reality of the psyche corresponds to the freeing of the captive and the unearthing of the treasure."

—Erich Neumann

MINING METAPHORS FOR ALL THEY'RE WORTH

Congratulations. You have now covered the nine basic developing questions and the problem/remedy/outcome strategic model. Way to go! You can accomplish extraordinary things with just these.

This last section of the workbook offers you tools, activities, and information to help you consolidate what you have learned. It will challenge you with client statements which do not break everything down for you into neat, easily manageable pieces where examples are crafted to suit the directions given. In other words, they are more like real client sessions.

But first...

Are there particular CLQs you are still struggling with? Now is a good time to go back and practice using them again before you take on the sort of complicated statements clients are likely to give you. Many of the practice activity examples can be used for other purposes than the one the directions give. You can also practice more with a partner with the goal of simply repeating their words accurately and listening for opportunities to practice the particular skill or question you need to work on.

I think you will also find revisiting the text portions of this workbook periodically after you have worked with Clean Language and Symbolic Modeling for awhile will reveal that information, suggestions, and insight that you may have glossed over the first time will have greater meaning for you with the new perspectives you gain as your skills and your experience with clients increase.

When you were learning to drive, you didn't drive on a busy road until you had the basic skills of accelerating, braking, changing lanes and the rest under your belt. Are you ready for traffic?

Time for more challenging stuff! I'm providing you with a few more charts that you may find useful. If they are helpful to you at this stage of your learning, great. Or, you may want to make a chart of your own to keep by your side. Everyone has their own best system for supporting their learning, which should come as no surprise now that you realize, on a deep level, how truly unique each individual is.

SAMPLE SESSION PROGRESSION

Desired Outcome: And what would you like to have happen?

Client: I want to feel more joy in my life.

Acknowledge: **And** you want to feel more joy in your life.

Focus attention: **And when** feel more joy,

Metaphor: That's joy like what?

Client: It's like dancing to a beautiful song instead of being a wallflower.

Acknowledge: **And** like dancing to a beautiful song.

Focus attention: **And when** dancing,

Attributes: **Is there anything else about that** dancing?

                   What kind of song **is that** song?

Location: **And whereabouts is that** dancing?

Time: **And when** dancing, **what happens just before** dancing?

                   And **when** dancing, **what happens next**?

Source: **And whereabouts could that** dancing **come from?**

Relationship: **And when** dancing to a beautiful song,
                   and when joy in your life,
                   is there a relationship between that dancing...
                   and more joy?

DEVELOPING A DESIRED OUTCOME LANDSCAPE

1. Establish a Desired Outcome

Problem	**And what would you like to have happen?**
Remedy	**And when [reworded remedy], then what happens?**
Desired outcome	**Developing questions**

2. Gather information about the Desired Outcome:

Metaphor	**And [x] that's like what?**
Attributes	**And what kind of/anything else about that [x]?**
Location	**And where/whereabouts could that [x] be?**
Time and Sequence	**And what happens just before [x]?**
	And then what happens?
Relationship	**And when [x] and when [y], is there a relationship between that [x] and that [y]?**
Source	**And where could that [x] come from?**

3. Think P/R/O:

Be listening for any additional problems, remedies, and desired outcomes that arise while developing information.

You may need to loop through the process again.

7.1 | *Activity*

Imagine your clients make the following statements, and you have all the time you need to think about them. (By the way, these are all quotes from my clients' sessions.) What would you want to find out about? Identify three things in each statement you would like to explore. What questions would you use? Use the charts on the previous pages to help you plan.

I think of my strategy as planning a few chess moves ahead; I think about where I want to direct my client's attention, always ready to change if they say something unexpected that invites a different strategy.

1. I want a relationship that's like having a dance partner.

2. It's like there's a cloud around my head, and I can't see where I want to go.

3. There are all these critical voices inside my head, and I want to get them out.

4. I'm lying on a blanket, and a group of people are tossing me in the air, effortlessly.

5. I really want to open up more, so my connections with others are more authentic.

6. I'm floating down a river, and there's a tree with light bark close to the bank. There aren't many of this type of tree, and I keep paying attention to this type.

7. There isn't a new boat in the harbor that's interesting enough that I'm willing to get on the new one and leave the old boat.

8. I'm looking for some kind of change, a revolution, but as inviting as that sounds, it also sounds intimidating. I could just stay in my nice little loop and carry on.

PREPARING A FIRST TIME CLIENT

If you already have a practice, no doubt you have your own process for meeting a client for the first time. What follows here are suggestions of a few ways you might want to modify or add to that process to prepare an adult client for a Symbolic Modeling experience. With younger clients who are not going to be reading a description or understand a lot of explanation, I simply suggest we play, and I usually stay with their drawings as we work.

Before the session: Not every client cares about this, particularly if they already know and trust you, but others want some ideas of what they're getting into ahead of time. I also email a *Before Our Session* sheet (See page 43) which I find helps the client collect their thoughts and helps us get into the meat of their work more directly. Clients often remark they have spent considerable time thinking about this one simple question, "And what would you like to have happen?" And then, of course, there are those who don't fill out the sheet, which is fine, too.

Situating: It's a rare client that isn't surprised by the first question, "And where would you like to be?" I encourage my client to experiment with their answer to that, to readjust their and my positions once we're seated, and to change them at any time as they become accustomed to the process. (Revisit page 40 for more reasons for this step in the process.)

Explaining the process: I refer to the description I provided and ask if the client has any questions. Depending on the age and interests of the client, I may go into a bit of detail about why using metaphors would make a difference and about brain neuroplasticity. (See page 21)

Setting up expectations: I make clear that I will not be maintaining eye contact as in a normal conversation and explain my reasoning for that. I stress this session is about their self- *exploration*, not self-*explanation*. I invite (not direct or tell) the client to feel free to close their eyes, suggesting that as their metaphor world comes alive for them, they may find they are in a slightly altered, inner-focused state.

I talk about how I will be asking questions about their *exact words*, as accurately as I possibly can, so they can hear their own words back, and notice what they notice. I explain that I will be taking copious notes so as to be able to use their exact words as best I can, that I am not labeling, diagnosing, or otherwise judging in any way, and that they are welcome to have a copy of my transcript notes. But I make no guarantees that they will be legible! If the client does want a copy, I take photos and text it to them, keeping the original for my files.

I encourage the client to feel free to direct my questions to what they sense is important or compelling; we are *co-facilitating*. Like dancers, I am usually in the lead, so they can concentrate on exploring and experiencing their metaphor world, while I am steering, keeping track, and thinking about connections, etc. But I am ready at any time to give over the lead briefly so they can redirect us, and then I will pick up the lead again. This is a client-centered process; ultimately, they are in charge.

I end the set-up with a final invitation to ask questions, and begin with asking the client to read what's on their *Before Our Session* sheet and describe their drawing(s).

| FAQ | *Frequently Asked Questions* |

What if I can't get my client into metaphor?

First ask yourself, what [x] word(s) were you asking the "And that's [x] like what" of? Was it an embedded metaphor, a word(s) that implied an image or object was there, just below the surface? Hopefully, if you are asking the questions about a word like *bubbling* or *radiating* that suggests an object or image, you will not have a problem getting your client into their metaphor landscape. But for some first time clients, opening up to an emerging image or other sort of metaphor that is not cognitively chosen may take a bit of getting used to.

I want to assure you that the more you practice Clean Language, the better you are going to get at hearing those **embedded metaphors** that can *pass on by* so easily. (Would you have caught that one?) You will get better at noticing opportunities to get your client into their symbolic domain. Right now, you may be concentrating on listening for **resources** to develop and be thinking **P/R/O**, and it can be challenging to catch those subtler metaphoric words, but you will get there.

But sometimes, even if you're asking the invitation-to-metaphor question of a word that sounds like an implied metaphor to you, you may have clients who answer with more description, with adjectives. And this is fine, for it is certainly more information to work with. But at some point you want to get into those embodied metaphors. More cognitive descriptions, which tend to get lots of explanations thrown in, is not what you're going for.

I may prepare my new clients for the metaphor question ahead of time so that they are not as likely to be pulled out of their symbolic domains into cognitive problem solving to try to make sense of the question. I tell them I'll be asking, "And that's like what?," and I model the slow-paced way I'll be saying it, so it clearly doesn't sound like ordinary conversation. Your client will soon learn to hear that drawn-out question as a rhythmic cue that you are asking for a metaphor.

Despite asking questions of what I suspect are embedded metaphors and despite using my most obvious voicing and pacing of my "And that's [x] like what?" question, there are *still* times some clients go on and on with descriptions. Sometimes, I move on with them, waiting for another opportunity to segue into their metaphor worlds. And sometimes I'll ask, in as rhythmic a way as I can muster, using these very cognitive sounding words, **"And when [x], is there an image or a symbol...?"** and I just leave my sentence unfinished. With a client who is not used to "finding" their metaphors, I admit to resorting to this on occasion. I'm not encouraging this; I'm just trying to help you out as you learn. The better you get at spotting the embedded metaphors, the less likely you are to come up against this problem.

But sometimes, giving descriptions that analyze a situation is just the way clients are most used to talking to a professional. Or it's the way they interpret your "And that's like what?" question itself. They may need this reminder that you're looking for a metaphor. *Certainly, you don't want this "image/symbol" to become your standard question!! Clean Language questions should ideally use simple words that take very little cognitive processing.* Stick with Grove's exact wording except as a last resort.

I let my client know that, to find these metaphors, they don't have to have any special talent or skill or be particularly creative (though they may find it particularly fun if they are!) I also let them know there can be something of a learning curve for new clients, and they shouldn't be concerned if it takes them a few tries to get the hang of discovering information about their metaphors. I assure them everyone "gets it" by the end of their first session—and they do.

Or use the metaphor map the client made on the *Before Our Session* sheet, if you used one, or have them create one now. When a client puts something into a drawing, they *have* to be using symbols. Ask attribute questions of the map's symbols, and be working with P/R/O.

What if my client resists the idea of drawing?

Respect your client's wishes, and let it go for the time being. I find that once most clients are comfortable with the process, they become more open to drawing. Then again, some are never interested in drawing. It's your challenge to adjust to your client, not theirs to adjust to you.

What if my client doesn't know what I mean by, "And where/whereabouts is that [x]?"

If you ask your first *where* question about something that the client has clearly given you a hint they have location information about (i.e. they talk about [x] being *behind* them now, or, as they speak, they put their hand *on their chest or gut*), they will likely grasp what you're asking. Once they have done that a few times, they will likely be able to locate something less obvious, like "And where is that dancing?" (assuming, of course, that it has a location. If your question leads to a dead end, just ask something else.)

My questions:

7.2 | Activity

Make an outline of key points you would like to cover when you introduce a Clean Language session to your typical client.

7.3 | Activity

Practice again with a partner. Plan on having a 30 minute session. This will give you time to really discover a lot of information. Use the charts on pages 105 and 106 for help, whichever works best for you. Or create your own help sheet. Practice your introduction, as if you this was your first session with this client.

Are there particular strategies (like P/R/O) or questions (maybe Time or Source?) that you would like to focus on practicing in this session? Make a note of them here.

Afterwards, answer the following questions:

Something I did well was:

Something I want to work on next time is:

7.4	*Activity*

These are typical of the sort of statement a client makes at the beginning of a session. You will find some of these statements are pretty chatty. You need to be separating the wheat from the chaff, the relevant from the irrelevant. Eliminate the explanations. Think P/R/O. Make some notes about what your strategy would be so you can discuss this with other Symbolic Modelers.

1. I get so serious and task-driven. My wife says I'm a workaholic, and I do get tension headaches. She says I need to relax more, but I can't just sit around doing nothing! I like to be active. If only I could do that in a more relaxed way—more playful, maybe.

2. Lately I've been really testy around the office. Maybe it's the economy. I worry that every little criticism is a hint that the ax might fall! I'd like to feel more flexible about how I respond to situations. I just get defensive so quickly—like a knee-jerk reaction. Whatever happens, that's not helping matters!

3. I'd like to not allow my emotions to rule my actions or determine my mood. I'd like to be able to motivate myself. I'd like to find healthy ways to get out of difficult situations, not use food or TV/avoidness to cope with uncomfortable situations or emotions.

   (Wondering what should you do when a client uses a made-up word like avoidness? Repeat it back to them as they said it. You don't want them to feel you are correcting them, and maybe it holds special resonance for them as is. You could ask a CLQ about it. If they correct themselves, then fine, use the corrected word.)

4. I've found myself lately in a place where I'm really anxious when I'm talking to my husband when it's just the two of us. I'd like to feel I can stay calm and talk openly and honestly with him.

7.5 | Activity

Here are some statements from the first few minutes of a client session. Use these excerpts of the transcript to practice: What do you notice, and what would you ask?

(My questions are by no means the only ones you could ask or even one of the best next ones. They are simply here to give you a new statement to work with.)

1. Rachel: *I'm letting things happen to me instead of rolling with the ups and downs, and moving on.... It's fear, I avoid it, and I just sit there. I want to get over the fear, not being scared, not letting the fear control me.*

2. Facilitator: And when moving on, that's moving on like what?

   Rachel: *Like climbing a mountain. Not being afraid of the ascent. Obstacles may come, and I'll know I can cope.*

3. Facilitator: And when know you can cope, what kind of cope is that cope?

   Rachel: *I can cope by taking action towards resolving it. Figuring out a way to fix it. I can cope if I'm open to learning. When I'm not fearful of what could happen— living in the moment. Rolling with the punches.*

7.6 | *Activity*

Underline the embedded metaphors. Label **P**roblem, **R**emedy, and **D**esired **O**utcome statements. Start strategizing: Circle words/phrases you'd want to explore with your client.

1. I'm thinking about retiring. My pension is adequate to sustain me. I don't have to worry about that. And it would be a sizable relief not to have worries about meeting my sales quota or rallying my sales team. But what will I do with myself? I read these books…I ask myself, "How will I feed my soul?" I've defined myself by my work for 40 years. Who am I without my job? How will people picture me?

2. I've injured my back repeatedly in recent months. My lower back gets tight and inflexible. Then I'm not sure if I should exercise gently—or what's gentle enough—or should I coddle it and let it rest? You know, my mother has a history of back problems, but then she's very overweight. I don't want to be sitting on the sidelines like her when I get older. She's sort of not on the active roster anymore, if you know what I mean. In fact, it seems like my back feels worse after I've spent some time with her.

3. I want to exercise regularly, but I hate it! I get bored easily and don't stick with it. Some people say exercising energizes them, but for me, it's draining, so it's tough to get psyched to take the initiative to get started actually doing it. There's a part of me that just says, "Oh, whatever. Forget it." or "Maybe tomorrow." I keep putting it off. But I know, in my head, that I need to get cracking!

4. I've got a real problem with clutter. I realize I'd be more efficient if I cleaned it up, but I get overwhelmed when I think about it! Or I start, and after spending two hours at it, I've accomplished so little, I get discouraged. I'll never get out from under this mountain of stuff! It's not like it's all trash; some of it could come in handy in the future.

APPLYING CLEAN LANGUAGE AND SYMBOLIC MODELING

No doubt as you made your way through this workbook, you have been thinking about, if not already incorporating, Clean Language and Symbolic Modeling into the work you do with clients. Perhaps you have even introduced bits of it into your conversations with family, friends or work colleagues. These are rich and flexible tools you will find many ways of using. Consider the following applications:

Who Can Use These Skills?

Health care: counselors, therapists, acupuncturists, doctors, nurses, energy healers
Coaches: life, executive, transitions
Families: couples, parents and teens
Businesses: employee-employers, teams, marketing and sales reps, leaders/managers
Education: school counselors, teachers, administrators, students
Interviewers: detectives, researchers, journalists
Group or community facilitators, mediators
Creative artists

USING CLEAN LANGUAGE CONVERSATIONALLY

You needn't limit your use of Clean Language to times when you are working with your client's metaphors. You don't even need to use the exact phrasing of the CLQs. You can artfully use Clean concepts, what we call maintaining a Clean stance.

Think Clean!

- Listen mindfully.
- Avoid assumptions.
- Ask the person you are speaking with to explain just what they mean by certain terms or concepts. Keep getting more details.
- Repeat some key words or phrases exactly
- Mix Clean Language questions in with other responses.
- Acknowledge the speaker's metaphor, and frame your response using its attributes and logic.

Think P/R/O!

- Rather than argue the problem, ask the person what they would like to have happen or what they would like it/things to be like.
- Don't stop at a remedy. Keep asking for a desired outcome.

Conversational *Clean* Questions

Ask Clean questions in a more natural, conversational way:

Example: What's that like for you?
             What would it be like if it was how you wanted it to be?
             Can you say more about that?

Notice how you can avoid phrases like 'think about' or 'feel about', leaving it more open-ended as to where the speaker goes for a response—head, heart, gut, or elsewhere. There is different information in each place.

Avoid phrases with "I" or "me" in them. However subtly, you are inserting yourself into the speaker's exploration.

Example.   I want to know more about that
             Tell me more about that...
             I don't really get it...
             That's interesting... (bringing attention to its interest to *you*)

7.7 | Activity

People around the world are using Clean Language and Symbolic Modeling in creative ways. How do you envision using it?

What's Next

YOUR OWN SYMBOLIC MODELING SESSION

If you haven't already experienced a personal, full-on Symbolic Modeling session (by which I mean being facilitated by someone fully trained in the method), this is a good next step to fully appreciate what the full process feels like and can do. You can arrange for a sample session by contacting me at gina@cleanlanguageresources.com or searching the Internet for other certified Clean Language practitioners.

BASICS PART TWO: FACILITATING CHANGE

After you have facilitated a client to gather information about an issue, a resource and/or landscape, what can you do with Symbolic Modeling to assist your client, when greater clarity alone hasn't brought about the change they are seeking?

That is what I cover in the next workbook in this series, including...

- Specialized Questions to further develop a landscape
- An emphasis on modeling strategy—what to ask when and why
- More practice activities
- How to establish conditions for change
- How to facilitate change
- How to concretize change
- More advanced working with resources, the basic questions, desired outcomes, etc.
- Distinguishing between coaching and counseling with Symbolic Modeling

Mining Your Client's Metaphors: A How-To Workbook on Clean Language and Symbolic Modeling, Basics Part Two: Facilitating Change is available at Amazon and major online book retailers.

TRAINING

Visit https://www.cleanlanguageresources.com/clean-language-workshops for information about my online and in-person training workshops and practice groups. If nothing convenient for you is on the calendar, let me know of your interest by contacting me at gina@cleanlanguageresources.com

Resources

Symbolic Modeling was developed by Penny Tompkins and James Lawley, based on David Grove's Clean Language methodology. You can learn more about them and the process at www.cleanlanguage.co.uk. The site is rich in resources. It includes over 200 articles written by people using Symbolic Modeling and Clean Language in a multitude of ways. It functions as the heart of the international Clean community.

There are several Facebook groups for Clean Language community members. Clean Language Open Community has over 1,400 members. It's a great place to connect with Clean enthusiasts from all over the world.

RECOMMENDED READING

About Clean Language and Symbolic Modeling

Campbell, Gina. *Mining Your Client's Metaphors: A How-To Workbook on Clean Language and Symbolic Modeling Basics Part Two: Facilitating Change.* Balboa Press (Bloomington, IN, 2013; reprint 2021)

Campbell, Gina. *Panning for Your Client's Gold: 12 Lean Clean Language Processes.* Balboa Press (Bloomington, IN, 2015)

Campbell, Gina. *Hope in a Corner of My Heart: a healing journey through the dream-logical world of inner metaphors.* Balboa Press (Bloomington, IN, 2018)

Cooper, Lynn and Castellino, Mariette, *The Five-Minute Coach: Improve Performance Rapidly.* Crown House Publishing (Wales, 2012)

Dunbar, Angela, *Clean Coaching: the insider guide to making change happen.* Routledge (Oxon and New York, 2017)

Harland, Philip, *Trust Me, I'm the Patient.* Wayfinder Press (London, 2012)

Lawley, James and Tompkins, Penny, *Metaphors in Mind: Transformation through Symbolic Modelling.* The Developing Company Press (London, 2000)

Pole, Nick, *Words that Touch: How to Ask Questions Your Body Can Answer (12 essential 'Clean questions' for mind/body therapists).* Singing Dragon (London, 2017)

Sullivan, Wendy and Rees, Judy, *Clean Language: Revealing Metaphors and Opening Minds*, Crown House Publishing, Ltd. (Wales, 2008)

Way, Marian, *Clean Approaches for Coaches: How to Create the Conditions for Change with Clean Language and Symbolic Modeling*. Clean Publishing (Hampshire, England, 2013)

About Metaphors

Geary, James *I is an Other: The Secret Life of Metaphor and How It Shapes the Way We See the World,* Harper Collins Publishers, (New York, 2011)

Kopp, Richard R. *Metaphor Therapy: Using Client-generated Metaphors in Psychotherapy,* Brunner/Mazer, (Bristol, PA, 1995)

Pinker, Steven, *The Stuff of Thought: Language as a Window into Human Nature,* Penguin Books, (New York, 2007)

Zaltman, Gerald and Zaltman, Lindsay, *Marketing Metaphoria: What Deep Metaphors Reveal About the Minds of Consumers*, Harvard Business Press (Boston, 2008)

References and Footnotes

SECTION TITLE PAGE QUOTATIONS

Section One: Sigmund Freud (1856–1939)
Section Two: Diane Ackerman (1948–) *Deep Play* (New York: Random House,1999)
Section Three: From "Finding What You Didn't Lose" by John Fox, copyright ©1995 by John Fox. Used by permission of Jeremy P. Tarcher, an imprint of Penguin Group (USA) Inc.
Section Four: T. S. Eliot (1888–1965) from "Little Gidding," Quartet No. 4, V
Section Five: Viktor Frankl (1905–1997) *Man's Search for Meaning* (Boston: Beacon Press, 2006)
Section Six :Carl Jung (1875–1961)
Section Seven: Erich Neumann (1905–1960)

FOOTNOTES

1. See Seigel, Daniel, M.D. *Mindsight: A New Science of Personal Transformation*, Bantam Books, (New York, 2011); see p.40.

   Here are a few other suggestions about where to go to read about neuroplasticity and therapies: Cozolino, Louis, Ph.D. The Neuroscience of Psychotherapy: the Social Brain, W.W. Norton & Co. (New York, 2010); Doidge, Norman, M.D. The Brain that Changes Itself, Penguin Books (New York, 2007); Hanson, Richard, Ph.D. Buddha's Brain, New Harbinger (Oakland,CA, 2009); Yapko, Michael, Ph.D. Mindfulness and Hypnosis: The Power of Suggestion to Transform Experience, W.W. Norton (New York, 2011)

   While Milton Erikson did not use the term neuroplasticity, he believed in the need for the client to experience the resourceful skills he needs and bring that experience to the problem context in order to change and grow. (O'Hanlon, William Hudson and Martin, Michael, Solution-Oriented Hypnosis: An Eriksonian Approach, W.W. Norton & Co. [New York,1992], p.136)

2. Tell all the Truth, poem #741 by Emily Dickinson

Answers to Activities

ANSWERS FOR ACTIVITY 1.2

1. I was <u>under</u> the <u>impression</u> that my <u>contact</u> had <u>set up</u> the interview ahead of time.
2. I <u>found</u> my <u>footing</u> once I <u>went to greater lengths</u> to practice regularly.
3. Now that I'm <u>fully</u> retired, I'm eager to <u>have</u> more <u>time</u> in my life for creative pursuits.
4. Is the whole idea <u>behind</u> this technique to help keep facilitators <u>out of</u> their clients' <u>inner worlds,</u> or to get them <u>in</u>?
5. I <u>strengthened</u> my resolve, and made real progress <u>moving forward</u>.
6. Clean Language is a <u>flexible</u> <u>tool,</u> <u>invaluable</u> in any professional's <u>toolbox</u>.
7. The new teacher's <u>quick</u> mind and curiosity <u>energized</u> her students.
8. I <u>carry</u> a <u>ton</u> of responsibility <u>on my back</u>!

As different people will respond differently to the same word, some words will evoke a metaphor for some individuals and not for others. You may or may not agree with me about the choices above, or you may identify some I have not. What's important is not that you get these all "right," but that you develop an ear for possible embedded metaphors your clients use.

ANSWERS FOR ACTIVITY 1.3

1. Every night when it's time for homework, there's a <u>battle</u> with my boys. If they're not arguing with me, they're arguing with each other. It's like it's a <u>contest</u> to <u>get</u> my attention, and once they <u>have</u> it, all they want to do is complain. They really <u>push my buttons</u>, and I'm at my wit's end!
2. I went to college thinking I was going to <u>pursue</u> a degree in math,but I've done an <u>about-turn</u>, and my father's not happy with me. I <u>discovered</u> I am really <u>drawn to</u> theater, and he's sure I'll be a <u>pauper</u> the <u>rest of</u> my life. He's threatening to <u>cut me off</u>, not pay my tuition. I don't want to be <u>left high and dry</u> or <u>saddled</u> with a <u>boatload</u> of loans! I'm not sure how to <u>approach</u> him now.
3. I've been working <u>under</u> bosses all my life. I want to <u>strike out</u> on my own! I know it's a <u>gamble</u> and it'll be a lot of <u>hard</u> work, but I want to open an Internet cafe in my town. You know, sort of a neighborhood <u>watering hole</u>, like on that old TV show Cheers, but without the beer.
4. Playing sports has always been a <u>huge part</u> of my life, and being an athlete a <u>big part</u> of my identity. I've always felt people <u>saw</u> me as <u>larger than life</u>, you know? And that <u>gave</u> me confidence. But now... with this injury..., that's all going to change. I'm not <u>that person</u> anymore. Who am I now? Where do I <u>fit in</u>?

ANSWERS FOR ACTIVITY 2.1

1. I'm very <u>efficient</u> at running meetings.
2. I want to <u>balance</u> my work and play.
3. I feel a <u>ball of energy</u> in my gut that starts <u>glowing</u> when I get on the court.
4. I'd like to access the <u>feeling</u> that <u>everything I need</u> is already there waiting for me.
5. I want my success to <u>flow naturally</u> and <u>easily</u>.
6. My professor's so <u>welcoming</u> of our ideas. It gives me the <u>confidence</u> to speak up in class.
7. If I <u>push myself</u> harder, I'm sure I can win <u>his trust</u>. (Is the pushing resourceful? Is it good thing? A bad thing? Since it's a matter of the client's perspective, sometimes you only know by asking. More on this in Section 5. For now it's great if you just notice the possibility that being able or motivated to push oneself might be a resourceful state.)

There are other words you could arguably label as resources. Does the client suggest these things are valued? Discuss them with your practice buddy. The point is not to be right; it's about developing your ear for resources in your client's language as it flies by.

ANSWERS FOR ACTIVITY 2.5

1. I want to be at <u>the top</u> of <u>the top</u> of the class.
2. I'm really <u>drawn</u> to more <u>exploring</u> of possible new renewable energy sources.
3. I want to <u>go easy</u> on myself when I am learning something new.
4. As I <u>picture</u> my future now, it's <u>full steam</u> ahead.
5. We're <u>working towards</u> reconciliation.
6. I want to make a <u>solid</u> commitment to our life together.
7. I'm wondering how I can be <u>playful</u> even when I am working.
8. I want to get my temper <u>under my control</u>.
9. When I get home from work, I want to <u>leave it behind</u> and be <u>fully present</u> for my family.
10. I would like to be able to <u>stand up to</u> my grandfather when he bullies my mother.

ANSWERS FOR ACTIVITY 3.1

1. I want to <u>feel confident about my decisions</u>.
2. I want my <u>energy to flow freely</u> and evenly.
3. I want to be <u>able</u> to <u>think about the future</u> in a more hopeful way.
4. I wish I could <u>hold on to an insight</u> and <u>run with it</u>.
5. I need to <u>find a new source of motivation</u>.
6. I would like a <u>better work-life balance</u>.
7. If only I could to <u>trust my feelings</u>.
8. I'd love to be <u>comfortable in my own skin</u>!
9. I want to <u>convey to my clients</u> that I really care about their problems.

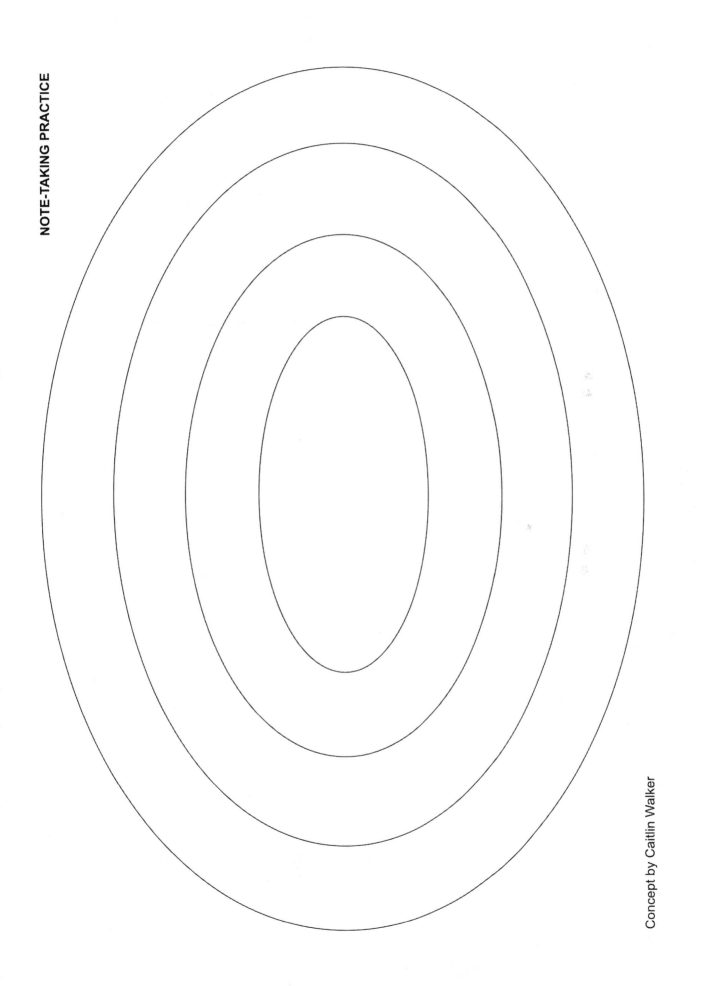

Concept by Caitlin Walker

Glossary of Terms

attributes: characteristics of an object, person, place, etc.

backtracking: a facilitator repeats previously given information in reverse order to smoothly direct the client's attention to a previously used word or image in order to ask a question about it.

choice point: a moment or place at which a client has the opportunity to choose among options.

clean: refers to when a facilitator uses primarily a client's exact words and gestures and adheres to the inherent logic of their metaphors. Thus, a "clean question" uses only a bare bones structure of words that are not the client's, and "staying clean" means the facilitator offers no advice, interpretations, or alternative perspectives.

Clean Language: the special questions and syntax originally developed by counseling psychologist David Grove to encourage clients to explore their metaphors and inner worlds in order to better know themselves.

Clean Language Syntax: the word order/wording of a Clean Language question. What is called full syntax consists of three parts: the repetition of the client's words for acknowledgment, the narrowing down of those words to the ones their attention will be directed towards, and the question itself.

Desired Outcome: what the client wants and does not currently have.

embedded metaphors: words that suggest an image, object or comparison not immediately noticeable to most people. Words that may have originally been easily spotted as overt metaphors have become so familiar that we easily overlook their references to other experiences. (Ex. She noted the cap he had on. It's beyond comprehension.)

embodied metaphors: these metaphors compare one thing to something experienced by a physical being in a physical world. They refer to body, sensor and/or spatial experiences. (Ex. I want to *get over* my disappointment and *move on*. He has a lot of responsibilities to *shoulder*.)

Explanations: the stories and analyses a client offers about the who, what, whys, etc. of their situation and themselves, which may or may not be accurate or relevant.

gestural metaphors: metaphors suggested by body movements.

"invitation to metaphor": the facilitator asks a Clean Language question that asks for a metaphor for a feeling, gesture, experience, etc. that a client introduces. ("And that's like what?")

"logic of the landscape": refers to the idiosyncratic characteristics of a client's metaphors and their interactions. Each client's landscape of metaphors has its own rules and processes, which may or may not coincide with our daily, earthly logic. (Ex. If a heart is surrounded in ice, heat may melt the ice... or simple awareness of the ice could melt it, or a vibration, etc.)

internalized metaphors: largely subconscious metaphors that encode a client's experiences and their interpretations of them.

looping: a return to a previous stage in the modeling process. Example: a client may determine a desired outcome, only to come back to the same or another problem or remedy. Also refers to a client's movement back and forth among the 5 stages of the Symbolic Modeling process, rather than moving sequentially from Stage 1-5.

metaphor: a comparison of two unlike things that share one or more qualities or characteristics; a description of one thing or experience in terms of another. In Clean Language, the term is used to encompass parables, similes, analogies, and the like.

metaphor landscape: the sum total of a client's symbolic images as they relate to one another.

metaphor map: a client's depiction of their metaphors as they relate spatially to one another, like locations on a map.

modeling: the process of developing a model of the client's internal world, which may include their internalized metaphors. Modeling entails using a variety of strategies to help a client discover and experience their symbols, their interactive relationships, and patterns.

natural trance: an hypnotic state induced by conversational guidance (as compared to a formal, scripted induction.) A deeply self-reflective state; a state of mindful inner focus with easier access to the subconscious.

neuroplasticity: the brain's capacity to be flexible, to change, to grow new neurons and new connections between neurons. Necessary for learning.

overt metaphor: the comparison of a person, place or thing to another is quite obvious to both the listener and the client. (Ex. Our negotiations have reached a *dead-end*.)

psychoactive space: a term coined by David Grove to describe a place or space filled with information from the client's inner experience with which they actively engage.

remedy: a client's desire to have less of a problem. Thus, the statement includes both their problem and their want. What will result from a remedy is not described.

REPROCess: acronym for Resource, Explanation, Problem, Remedy, Outcome, Change and -*ess* for reprocessing itself.

reviewing: the facilitator verbally repeats multiple words and images to help the client keep a large piece of their metaphor landscape in their conscious awareness, generally in anticipation of asking a question about it all or to bring closure to a session.

resource: that which a client identifies as being helpful or of some value to them.

resource state: a feeling or state of being that, once achieved, will help a client do what they want to do or change what they need to change.

resource symbol: a symbol or metaphor which is helpful to a client in some way.

self-modeling: when a client explores their inner world for themselves, discovering new information about its elements and/or metaphors and their relationships and patterns.

scope of practice: refers to the appropriate clients and issues a professional facilitator should take on, given their training, experience, and the contract of services to be provided.

symbolic domain: a client is described as being "in their symbolic domain" when they are in an inner-focused, mindful state, exploring and experiencing their internalized metaphors. We say they "leave the symbolic domain" when they return to an alert, fully conscious awareness of their surroundings; they are no longer engaged with their metaphors in an experiential way.

Symbolic Modeling : a language-based, mind/body process that invites a client to achieve greater clarity about any personal topic, including themselves, and to work through problems at a very deep level. It uses 3 elements: Clean Language, metaphors, and modeling.

systems thinking: approaching a whole (such as a person or organization)as an interactive system of parts. In linear thinking, the emphasis is on how one part influences another part (cause and effect.) Systems thinking pays particular attention to the feedback the effecting parts get, and how they respond in turn.

MINING YOUR METAPHORS
Change the metaphor, Change the Self

Gina Campbell, Director and Trainer

visit **www.cleanlanguageresources.com**
and keep up to date on what's happening!

Sign up for our newsletter and learn about the latest...

Training opportunities
Online courses
New publications
Clean applications

...and more

Join Mining Your Metaphors on...

Facebook
and
LinkedIn

...for links to articles of interest.

Using this workbook to teach others? Request a free copy of

*The Trainer's Guide to How-To Workbooks
on Clean Language and Symbolic Modeling Parts I and II*

Send an email to
gina@miningyourmetaphors.com